MEMORY T

Memory Games and ____ __.ning
to Improve Memory and Prevent
Memory Loss

–

Mental Training for Enhancing
Memory and Concentration and
Sharpening Cognitive Function

EDOARDO
ZELONI MAGELLI

ISBN: 9798622803178 - March 2020 - Original Version: Allenamento per la Memoria: Giochi di Memoria e Allenamento Cerebrale per Prevenire la Perdita di Memoria – Allenamento Mentale per Migliorare la Memoria, la Concentrazione e le Funzioni Cognitive

Author: Psychologist, Businessman and Consultant. Edoardo Zeloni Magelli, born in Prato in 1984. In 2010, soon after graduating in Psychology of Work and Organizations, he launched his first startup. As a Businessman he is CEO of Zeloni Corporation, a training company specialising in Business Applied Mental Sciences. His company is a reference point for anyone who wants to realize an idea or a project. As a scientist of the mind he is the father of Primordial Psychology and helps people to strengthen their minds in the shortest possible time. A music and sport-lover.

UPGRADE YOUR MIND → zelonimagelli.com

UPGRADE YOUR BUSINESS → zeloni.eu

CONTENTS

"Memory decreases if you don't exercise it."

MARCUS TULLIUS CICERO

Introduction

Our brain is probably the most precious organ that we have. It holds everything that we value the most. It keeps info stored about our most beloved friends and family members. We cherish beautiful memories of the best moments of our lives and even the darkest ones. We also keep the very valuable lessons that prevent us from repeating the same mistakes.

What a wonderful organ our brain is! But unfortunately there are some mental abilities that already begin to decrease after the age of 25. One of these is memory. This is alarming considering that our life expectancy is continuously increasing.

We live in a world that is getting us used to using our brains less and less. The automated services, modern comforts and new technologies that do the work for us are making logical thinking obsolete. Technologies can also improve your life, but many of them are rushing your mental abilities. If you continue to neglect your memory and do nothing to maintain your mental faculties, your cognitive decline will come soon. Don't wait to grow old to pay more attention to your mental health. Use the important tools in this book before it's too late.

Fortunately, the brain can be trained and there are skills that can improve even at the age of 70. On the next pages you will find tools, activities, techniques, games, exercises and tips that will help you significantly improve your brain's performance.

It is important to start undertaking activities that will stimulate you intellectually if you want to stay awake and active even in old age. The more we stimulate our brain, the easier it is for us to remember things. When you exercise, your brain structure changes, gray matter grows and white matter improves.

The first one performs the thinking and calculating activities and is a tissue that includes the bodies of neurons, dendrites and unmyelinated nerve fibers. It will provide you with a better basis for future learning processes as it performs the function of selecting and starting the information.

The second one, made up of myelin-coated axons, controls the signals shared between neurons and will help you optimize the exchange of information in the brain areas. The connections will therefore work better and be faster.

You don't need to be a doctor to understand that if you start training your brain, you will also improve in many other aspects of your life.

With great amazement you will discover that you will be even happier. Memory affects our expectations and attitudes. A good memory makes you happier and increases self-confidence. Studies have shown that brain exercises also have very positive effects on depression.

In short, by training your memory, you will also train your cognitive functions and improve the decision making and problem solving process. But there is more! You will increase the speed of information processing, you will also learn to reduce distractions to stay focused on what's important and you will become more aware of what surrounds you so that you can remember it better. This will also help you manage and reduce your stress levels.

After high school graduation, we become responsible for our education and personal growth. Most people stop exploring the world after they get a diploma or degree. Don't do like them. Don't be afraid to learn something new! Stop avoiding challenges and come back to life with a childish curiosity, you will learn much more than you can imagine.

Are you ready to start? We have only one brain and it's time to take care of it in the best possible way!

1. Techniques and Memory Improvement

Have you ever found yourself asking others to remind you to do something? Maybe you know that person you can always count on because you're sure he remembers every detail. Some people seem to have better memories than others. It may seem that memory is something obtainable at birth and that we cannot modify. However, that isn't true at all! There are no people with bad memory. There are people who make the most of their internal resources and others not.

Our memories serve a biological purpose. We need them to learn from our mistakes. If you never remembered that touching a hot pan could burn your fingers, you would be in pain frequently. If you didn't remember how to go to the bathroom, the world would be a lot messier of a place. Memories help us to grow and learn. We often remember the important things, such as how to drive or cook, but forget some of the more meaningful things, such as experiences with families or birthday of a beloved friend.

Memory is shown in animals, too. Your cat remembers that, when you bring the food bowl out, it means it's time to eat. Your dog recalls that, if he goes to the bathroom inside the house, you will get mad at him.

Animals keep memories that serve practical purposes. The same can be said for humans, but we also remember things for sentimental reasons. We remember the fun things, as well as what's important for our social lives, the little experiences that help define who we are and the people we know. It is also the memories we keep that differentiate us from other human beings.

Having a good memory serves a purpose. You can recite things that you know much easier. You can be that person who always knows everyone's name, asking small questions about their personal lives, such as how their newborn baby may be doing. You can remember important details to prove your point better. Besides, having a catalog of good memories can make the bleak days a little easier to get through.

Some people are ashamed of not remembering things well because they are considered not to be intelligent. But memory isn't associated directly with intelligence. Having a bad memory never means you're not intelligent!

We just need to work on memory enhancement. By learning the right techniques, you will improve your memory and learn better. You need constant practice and training if you want to keep your brain young and elastic. You will Increase your performance in study and work, and you will be able to efficiently memorize the information that interests you.

There are a few things you'll have to do to get an efficient memory. The first thing is to recognize that you are not taking advantage of your full potential and therefore you can do much more. The second is to become aware of your memory, what are your strengths and weaknesses? What are the things you can remember the most and which are the ones where you encounter the most difficulties?

Now focus on your habits. Are you currently doing things that can damage your memory? For example, eating nothing but junk food, drinking heavily and smoking cigarettes? It would be bad for your well-being for several reasons.

Don't forget that your habits influence your memory and your ability to understand and store information. The foods we eat, the lifestyle we live and the decisions we make have a direct effect on our memory. If you pay attention to these aspects, then it will be easier for you to have greater mental health overall. But these issues will be addressed in the third book of this series: *Memory Improvement*.

In this book, we will focus on memory training which - among the many benefits you will get - will also allow you to have an efficient memory. However, before that, let's discuss what an efficient memory even looks like. What is the high standard of a good memory? How can that be achieved naturally?

Memory Efficiency

Before we get into the fun and games, it's good to start with understanding what the standard for memory is. An efficient mind is can process information correctly. There are a few categories. There is the practical kind of things, e.g., your route to work, a doctor's appointment or the ingredients to a family recipe.

Then, there are the basic experience memories, such as the good times when you were laughing with friends, family, and the bad times that still hurt your heart and make you sad. After all of that, some moments tend to stick out the most. The lessons that we have learned. The smell of your lover's hair as they pull away from a kiss. The simple afternoon you spent alone in bed as the sun shone through the window. A random conversation you had with a stranger that made you smile. You likely have no issue remembering all of these incidents.

It's the doctor's appointments, the extra item on the grocery list, or the name of your boss's wife that, however, that you probably have trouble recalling. It is perhaps because they have less meaning to you. The taste of your grandma's pie, the first time you got your heart broken, the stray dog that scared you while you were walking alone in the street, these are all emotional memories. They are connected to something other than just a practical aspect of your mind.

It's the small and practical stuff that can be so hard to remember because it's simply not as important to us as the others. Where you have left your keys isn't going to take up space over other memories that you may be concerned with storing. But since there are so many practical and small things you need to know and keep in mind to live better, you need to find a way to increase your ability to retain this information.

Where can you start to improve the efficiency of your memory?

It is important that you start committing to new things. Everything you have done to date has led you to the situation where you are now, and you will not go further. Try out new activities. This is a process. It is just like working out your body. It is not an immediate solution. There isn't a pill that you can take to remember things better. Of course, there are some supplements that can help, as well as nutrition, however, the key to getting the best out of your body is within you. The trick to mastering your body is to actually use it and the tools that exist in you.

Make sure that you have a high mental clarity. This means that you need to cut out stressors and distractions. Think about when you get hurt. The first thing to do is to clean the wound. We are not saying that your "bad" memory is a wound; it's just an analogy that's easy for all of us to comprehend.

If you cut yourself with broken glass, you'd want to make sure you remove the glass splinters and put a Band-Aid on it to heal. Like a wound, you have to clean your mind out, remove distractions (stress), and focus on healing as you move forward.

Sleeping well is the basis for good mental clarity. Sleep is hugely important for having a healthy brain. Sleep is like recharging your brain's battery. It is one of the few organs that will absolutely never have a break. The brain doesn't sleep even when we sleep.

Even in the R.E.M. the electrical impulses of the brain are very intense. In fact, even when you sleep you can wake up and alert yourself if there is a threat. Think about when you are sleeping and suddenly a mosquito lands on your face. Without thinking about it, you automatically make a gesture to chase it away.

So the Brain is always active, both in the waking and sleeping phases. Only the electrical impulses and the way our brain establishes connections between neurons vary. In this way, it allows some cells and brain areas to rest. For example, when we sleep, areas are activated that facilitate the integration of information, the same that shape our long-term memory.

That is why it is so important to sleep well for our memory. If you want to start making your memory more efficient and want to make your brain work better, start respecting your biological clock. Make sure you sleep well.

To improve efficiency, you must also pay attention to

nutrition. You cannot have good intellectual and mental performance by eating badly. So the functioning of our memory is related to the food we eat.

Our brain feeds mainly on glucose, a molecule contained in food but also synthesized by the metabolism of carbohydrates, fats and proteins (Venuti, Marianetti, Pinna, 2018). When you eat unhealthy sources of these macronutrients, you're not nourishing your brain well. Stay away from refined foods and prefer organic food and preferably zero miles.

But don't forget that we're also made of water. To ensure proper brain function and keep your brain efficient over time, you also need to drink a lot. Water is the main constituent of the human organism. Two-thirds of our body are made up of water and over 80% of our brain is made up of water. Every chemical reaction that takes place in the brain needs it, including the production of energy in the brain. You can't have energy without water, it's your primary fuel. A minimal loss of water, such as a 3-4% decrease, can be enough to cause neurological symptoms such as clouded mind, fatigue, dizziness and confusion (Mosconi, 2018). That's why we need to drink a lot to have an efficient brain.

Habits are also important. For memory efficiency, we can't just do these things once to heal from mental fog. Implement the habits that I will discuss throughout the book as often as possible instead. Take the games that I'll be teaching and use them to make your life more fun and practical so that it can increase your memory.

In order for your brain to work properly, it needs to be in an environment of mental clarity. Reevaluate your situation and determine if there is something that gives you chronic stress and anxiety. Do you have the most stressful job ever, for instance? Are you constantly agonizing over your social life? Is there anything in your life that eats away at you on a daily basis? Confront these issues so that your brain has a chance to become clearer.

For your mental clarity, exercise is also important. It helps bring oxygen to the brain. There are many reasons why a healthy workout routine is important, but we have to remember that exercise keeps the brain active. So on your days, in addition to inserting a time slot for your mental training, remember to find time to exercise as well.

By improving your cognitive skills, you will also improve the learning and understanding of information. As a result, you will be able to better store new information.

To further improve your efficiency you often check your cognition (i.e. the acquisition of data related to a certain field, knowledge, awareness). How are you processing information? A negative mindset — one that is pessimistic and always assuming the worst — can be the result of several cognitive disorders. Confront these issues and find that your memory is starting to improve.

To conclude, always be inquisitive. Watch new things. Explore the world. Have a child-like perspective when approaching something that you don't understand. Be open to all that this world has to offer and relish the moment. Carpe diem.

The Cause of Being Forgetful

Many people are afraid when they forget something, but it is a natural process. This is not always a problem, sometimes it is a symptom of flexibility. When they accuse you of being distracted because you forget futile things, remind these people that memorizing and learning are two completely different things. Our brain eliminates all secondary information to make way for new information.

While long-term memory is potentially unlimited, short-term memory is a temporary memory that contains information only for a short period of time. Information that is not processed in short-term memory is not transferred to long-term memory and is therefore forgotten.

We forget things because our short-term memory is

limited. To make room for new information, we must necessarily delete other information. (Wimber, 2015). In fact, forgetting is a natural process that increases and speeds up our learning ability. So forgetting is an active process, it doesn't happen passively. It is no coincidence that the most active people, the most committed ones who are continually exposed to stimuli and new information, are the ones who most easily forget things.

So, remember, you'll always forget some things. Even as you actively work on improving your memory, there may be moments when you just can't hold onto information. Our brains are naturally prepared to store information, which means that they are also programmed to forget things as well. If we remembered everything we saw, we would be mentally exhausted. Imagine knowing the word to every song you've ever heard, even if it only happened once. You'd know every single first and last name of the people you've been introduced to, as well as what they're wearing. You'd remember the smallest details of movies, as well as the character names. You'd be able to recall things on the street, like a letter in the mailbox, a tiny branch that fell on the road, and the mother and her three children in a black stroller she's pushing.

While it would be nice to have such an efficient memory, a lot of this information is going to be useless. Your brain knows how to, and whether or not it should store certain ideas, as well as if it should just cycle them out.

We have two different types of memory: one that we have inherently and another one that we are taught to learn and form on our own. The inherent memory is based on who you are and what your personality may be. The environment where you have been raised will teach you what things are important and what are not. Such an experience will then tell your brain what it should hold onto and what is okay to push away.

For example, let's look at two different people. The first one, Maria, was raised in a very strict religious home. She was taught that women should be very modest and that being too outspoken could make you look bad.

Then, there was Jessica. Her home wasn't as strict as Maria's, but her parents put a huge emphasis on appearance. Everyone in the family always had to have perfect hair, flawless makeup, and the most stylish outfit.

Jessica and Maria are from the same city, but their families have really affected how they think and perceive the world. Then, one day, they meet a new girl named Ashley. Ashley has on a tight-fitting dress and is showing a lot of skin with styled hair and makeup that looks like it's done by a professional. She isn't afraid to swear or say what's on her mind as well.

Maria ends up remembering Ashley as someone who isn't very modest and has trouble controlling the things she says. Jessica, meanwhile, thinks of the opposite. She sees her a fashion icon, admires her style, and really looks up to her. She remembers Ashley as someone whom she envies and wishes to emulate.

These girls not only have different ways to perceive new information, but they have alternate ways of storing it as well. What you have gone through in your life has shaped how you'll take in and store information, after all. Think of how we physically store things as well. Some people would get an expensive action figure and keep it in the box for their entire lives. Then, others might take that action figure out right away and give it to their kids to play with. What we do in our physical lives will directly affect how we store and use information. And vice versa. Both consciously and subconsciously.

That's why we tend to forget some things and instead remember others.

What happens when we are extra forgetful is that we aren't making the proper connections in our brain. The key to learning new information is relating it to something that you already know.

Memory Tools

Your thought processes and how you work your brain are the most important things in your journey on memory improvement. You already have the tools needed inside of you to unlock the secret of being someone who remembers all the important things. And in your hands you have a manual that will help your memory blossom like never before.

There are a few tools that you will be able to use as well, including items that you can keep to make sure you're remembering new and important information more easily. The first one is a journal. You don't have to sit down and write a "Dear diary" entry every day, but take notes on your life. Not everyone is a scholar or someone who can eloquently write whatever thoughts or feelings they have, and that is okay. You don't have to write your autobiography. Just invest in a notebook that's around the size of your purse or pocket and keep it with you whenever possible. Write down reminders, keywords, and other small things that you can look at later and trigger a memory.

Having a smartphone or tablet is a nice bonus as well. A handheld electronic device will be rather useful to be able to have fun games and apps that will make learning easier. You can have a notes section on your phone to jot things down even when you don't have your journal with you, for instance. Some apps and sites will be discussed later on in this book so that you can have fun memory games with you at all times.

The idea is to try free apps before paying for anything. While some may promise that they can help with your brain power, there may not be legitimate studies to back up such a claim. The desire for a better memory is certainly a common wish among people all over the world, and many companies understand this. They will promise you brain strength with a paid subscription to their app, but you should not always buy into this. There are plenty of other free things that can still be helpful. Don't let someone exploit your desire for a stronger memory so that you have to pay out big and play a few games that you can find free versions of elsewhere.

Don't just stop at virtual games. There are also many physical games. Take as many as possible, such as the Rubik's cube, the Brussels cage and many more that you can find on the **upgradeyourmemory.com** website.

Also, invest in some sudoku, crossword puzzles, and word-search books. They have many of these at inexpensive places like gas stations or dollar stores, you can always take them with you to take advantage of downtime, such as work breaks, while you are queuing, traveling by train or plane.

Having a nice, quiet spot to meditate will also be helpful. If you have not meditated before, now is the time to start. Meditation allows you to cleanse yourself from external conditioning, to live in the here and now, to better observe reality. It serves to pull the plug, you will stop the continuous flow of thoughts that you have in your mind to relax it, to get in touch with the deepest part of yourself, in a state of tranquility. You will gain awareness and remove stress. A sunroom, terrace, quiet garden, or even just the spot on the floor at the end of your bed can be a great place to start meditating.

Learn and Memorize Better

By understanding your learning process, it will be much easier for you to memorize things. When learning something new, your brain will first pick up a sensory input, As we saw in the other book of this series, *Photographic Memory*, this is the first process of memory and is called encoding.

When you're reading a book for the first time, your brain starts to pull out the most relevant information and quickly start to store this. It will probably be based only what is emphasized to you, you may also find yourself catching information on to your individual perspective.

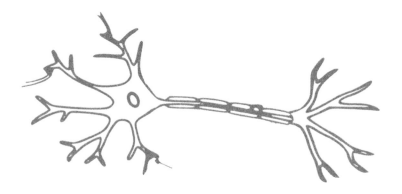

As you start to record new information, your brain is then going to start to make associations and connections to the things that you already know. This is why people react differently to the same event. Let's take an example.

Two people get fired from a company. These two people go back to their homes and tell their family members that they have just been fired from their jobs. One might react irrationally, crying and becoming very anxious about his future. The other may be able to remain calm, reflect, take time to understand what happened by bringing family members together and discussing what the next action should be.

Faced with new information, these people have come up to two different reactions. The first based his response on what he already felt: stress and anxiety over financial situations. The second also used his own experiences to know that difficult times can be overcome and that there's a light at the end of the tunnel. Understanding this process of association should help you. This is where you can start to manipulate your memories in your favor.

Not all new information will end up in your long-term memory. Remember that you will store information more easily if an important association takes place. Memory can also be weakened by the connections that we make. You have neurons in your brain that help to blend new and old information. We have a bad memory when our brains fail to do that, though. The brain is just like any other part of your body that you want to strengthen. You have to train him. If you are living a healthy lifestyle that's filled with the correct amount of sleep and exercise, then there are still a few more things you can do, and that's what we will be focusing on for the remainder of the book.

Here are some techniques and learning methods that you can use to store information more easily:

Move When You Learn Something

In addition to being a way to study without getting bored, it is also an activity that allows you to better assimilate concepts. For example, after every 25 minutes of study, do 5 minutes of exercise. You could do some free-body or stretching exercises. Or you can read while you walk.

When you connect the physical world to the mental information that you're taking in, then the idea will stick around longer. Moving facilitates the memorization of new concepts. Furthermore, this physiological activation keeps boredom and drowsiness away.

Making Associations

After you read something interesting that you want to remember, take a second and look at another object in the room. Even if it's just a throw pillow, for instance, connect the vision to it, and you will be able to recall that info later on more easily.

Ask Yourself

After you learn something, ask yourself some questions. This will facilitate a deep understanding and integration of the acquired knowledge.

Practice

After you've studied a topic, maybe after watching a

tutorial, put the information you've learned into practice right away. You learn and memorize it mostly by doing.

Teach Other People

As you learn more information, teach it to others, too. When you can teach, you can learn better. It is a way to repeat it.

Little Information at a Time

Don't overload yourself with new information. You won't remember much. Don't study superficially. It's better to study a little information at a time and go deeper.

Always dive deep into your brain to see the true meaning at all times. We will explore these topics further, but remember these techniques as you see more ideas in this book.

Strategies for Improving Memory

Focus

One of the most effective things ever is focus. Stay focused one thing at a time. Don't let your brain think about several things at once. So many things happen in this world that you might feel the need to gather as much information as possible. But the more data you absorb, the harder it will be to process the information.

There is so much happening in this world that the pressure to take in as much information as possible in any given moment is very strong. Remember that the more data you absorb, though, the harder it will be to process things one by one. You need to protect yourself from cognitive overload. The more you have to pay attention to, the less you can pay attention. The results come where you put your attention. So focus on one thing at a time.

"A wealth of information creates a poverty of attention."

Nobel Herbert Simon

When you're studying, for instance, don't watch TV at the same time. If you're writing, don't listen to music with words in it. Give your brain the opportunity to have the full, undivided attention that it need in order to remember things efficiently.

Organize everything that you are trying to learn. Put an emphasis on the most important ones to learn and focus on them first.

Reading Words Out Loud

Reading words out loud can be really helpful as well. It develops verbal intelligence, improves understanding, enhances language skills and improves mnemonic abilities because it exploits our auditory memory.

Here are some other ways to make sure that you are learning more easily and retaining information.

Make Changes

Change can be scary for many people. As animals, we want that haven because it means we'll be provided with food, shelter, and other forms of security. When things change, it means that our brains have new information to process. Many people facing a change feel less secure.

While change might be scary, always look for new ways to modify your life. This doesn't mean taking it in the complete opposite direction. There are small things you can do that will really help you to keep your mind active.

Change is helpful because you are learning and processing new information. You are forcing your brain to take in some things that it may already know, but force it to process it in a new way. When you do this, you are working out your brain. Again, think of it like losing weight. If you go for a 20-minute walk every day, that will certainly help you to lose weight. Eventually, however, the weight will stop coming off because your body becomes used to this regimen. Instead, you'd want to find different methods of exercise to keep your muscles active. You can do some weightlifting, leg-strengthening workouts, yoga, or even Pilates. Remember, you can do this with your brain! Always change things in order to process new information.

Do something different every day. Always try new things. When we were in school, we were often forced to do something new. For example, we worked on group projects with people we didn't know. We tried new games in the gym class. We had new teachers with new teaching styles every year. These experiences helped to keep our brains fresh and active, though. Once you're out of school, it can be easy to fall into a pattern of doing the same thing every day. For the brain, this behavior is not virtuous. Routine stifles the creativity of the intellect and lazes the vitality of the individual. Doing the same things over and over again, the brain tends to "shrink." Even if that's what your job calls for, there are still plenty of things that you can do differently every day to keep your mind alert.

A brilliant mind is not monotonous. Our brain works well if it's stimulated by new things. It's invigorated by using it like a muscle. Repetitiveness, on the other hand, makes it lazy, physically shrinks.

"Every habit is a bad habit."

François de La Rochefoucauld

Always Set Yourself New Goals

Ambition plays an important role in strengthening the desire for change. You must always have goals to achieve. Challenge yourself to create new horizons to reach. Change is good for life.

Always Learn More about Yourself

You don't have to be the same person forever. Always look for ways to expand your views. Question your morality, virtue, and ethics. Look deep within yourself to find greater truth and meaning. This doesn't have to be about religion, although it should be one aspect to look into. Overall, you should be based solely on you and who you are in this world.

Introduce Small Changes in Your Life

Change starts in small ways as well. Just change the hand you normally use to brush your teeth, or change the route to work. On the next few pages you'll find a whole section dedicated to exercises like these.

Have the courage to change. You will find yourself stronger.

Repetition

Repetition is the opposite of change! In small ways, however, it can be really helpful. Repeat healthy habits every day. Repeat the things that you do in order to improve your memory. This isn't a one-and-done kind of thing. You will need to actively work on increasing your memory every day.

Repetition will be useful in learning new information. When you realize something brand-new, write it down or say it out loud. This repetition will help to keep the idea sorted in your brain more easily.

2. Brain Training Activities for Better Memory

Aside from the lifestyle you partake in, it's also essential to try brain training activities to help you get an even better memory. Games aren't just for kids! These are good activities that help us in training. Before we get into those, however, we're also going to discuss actual exercises that you can start to implement into your brain training processes.

One way that you need to start to train your brains is through the process of listening. Even as you are reading these texts, it may be difficult to keep up with what we are saying because there are other background distractions. Noises from neighbors, maybe someone walking around in the kitchen, or a loud thunderstorm may all be distracting you at the moment. In order to really listen, it's essential to get rid of all these things so that we can put our attention on everything that we need the most.

When you are listening, repeat what the other people is saying to yourself. Instead of trying to find a deeper meaning or come up with a solution to what they're saying, go over the actual words they state as they come out of their mouths. Do this because it will help you become a better listener for the people who need an open ear.

We often spend our time prepping the response we're going to have rather than sitting there and listening to what someone says. Others don't really need anything from us in the conversation either and simply want to feel as though they are being heard.

Another great brain training activity is to pick out a new thing that you have learned that day. Some days, it will be greater than others, but there will always be a lesson that you can find in every situation. This causes you to analytically cycle through your day. Even if you didn't leave your house, you learned something that day. Maybe it was an interesting article that you read online, or perhaps a personal lesson that you learned through self-discovery. Whichever it may be, there is always at least one thing from your day that you can pull out as a lesson that you have learned.

This is a good thing to do in the morning as well. Pick out five things that you are grateful for. Take a minute to reflect on your life. Enjoy your morning brain-boosting smoothie while you reflect on the dawn. Take some time in the shower while you get ready to go to work and think about where you're going. When you can start your day fresh and energized, internally and externally, it will help increase your cognition throughout the day. Such activities not only help you to be more aware in the moment but increase your level of positivity towards a certain situation as well. Just like how a trainer may guide you to do several sets of push-ups a day, this book will help you to exercise your brain.

Basic Memory Exercises

The first way to help you remember something is through visualization. It can be rather challenging to recall new information because we only hang onto the words that we're learning. Whatever information that you're actually learning, though, visualize it in a solidified way. Look for examples to relate ideas to the things that you're discovering as well. If you're meeting some people for the first time, and you have trouble remembering names, visualize them saying their own names after they've introduced themselves.

Visualize what you might take with you if you were

going on a spontaneous trip. This activity will help you start to develop brain images. Let's say that someone called you and said that he had a free round-trip ticket to your favorite vacation spot, but you should be ready to go within 10 minutes if you wanted to make the trip. What would you take with you then? Which items would you focus most on throwing into a suitcase? These are just small examples of visualization exercises.

To stay focused on what you have to do, you have to resist distractions. Keep gum or mints with you. Not only do these keep your breath fresh, but they keep you focused as well. When you are studying, having gum or mints or some other candy (sugar-free!) that you can suck on for a longer period can keep you focused. Your main point of attention will be on the material that you're studying. After that, your brain will be concentrating on what you're eating, so rather than your brain drifting away somewhere else and losing focus, it will stay homed in on the important information. Studies have shown that chewing gum can momentarily increase concentration because it increases the oxygen supply to the brain.

Tap on your arm when you learn something new. Take your finger and rub it gently on your palm. Touch your forehead or tuck your hair behind your ears. Whatever this small touch may be, the physical connection with yourself can help you to remember information easier. When you learn something new, you can give your arm a quick tap so that you can recall it later on. When you have trouble recalling that information you attempted to store, you can touch yourself in the same manner to try and remember something.

Force laughter more often. Laughing provides positive energy to the brain, reduces stress hormones and increases endorphins. Serotonin is also released. Furthermore, when you laugh, the gamma frequencies inside your brain increase, and this leads to an improvement in concentration and memory.

Sit straight. Your posture is important for your

health, especially for your mental state. When you feel yourself slouching, force yourself to sit up straight. This will keep you alert and bring you back into the moment. It's okay if your back is not totally straight all the time. The important thing is that we are mindful of how we're sitting and able to quickly and easily correct it when we need to do so.

Map Drawing Game

Now I'm going to tell you about a very funny and also very old game. Drawing maps. Since ancient times, the map has been an essential communication tool. Man has always felt the need to describe the characteristics of a place or show how to reach it. Think of Egyptian papyrus, Renaissance maps but also prehistoric engravings.

Map drawing is a great way to help us recall our memories. It is a fun and challenging activity that can entertain you when you are bored, as well as help you recall the most relevant details. It doesn't matter what you use to draw your map. You can start with a large piece of paper and draw it just from memory using colored pencils. You can study a map first before drawing and do something more elaborate. You can also paint the map or even make a three-dimensional version using clay models and other fun structures. Whatever medium you choose is entirely up to you.

Draw a map of your home. This is a good place to start. Without looking up a blueprint, take a moment to sit down and sketch out your house. Just make sure you're doing it from a bird's-eye view. Keep it simple and give yourself a few different tries to get it right.

Create a map of your hometown as well. Even if you haven't been there in years, can you sketch out the basic layout of what your hometown looks like? Where are the streets? What hidden things are on certain roads? What are the biggest landmarks?

What about your childhood home, can you draw this from memory, too? What labels can you put on certain rooms? Rather than labeling the kitchen as such, what has happened here that you can label the room with? As you start to draw more and more from memory, you will awaken the hidden thoughts that you've had. It's like opening a book. You blow the dust off and start to skim through pages, remembering obvious things but also discovering that you remember a lot more than you realize.

Keep these maps in a journal as they can help you to store information in your mind better. It will allow you to understand certain things from your memory that may have confused you before as well. You will work out ideas and other important details mentally as you travel throughout these maps.

You can look at the maps to recall different memories. Maybe you're trying to think of a time as a child and what happened then. If you look at the map, it can help you to be visually there. As you draw more and more maps, it will become much easier to know what things are important to draw are.

Do you also want to try drawing maps of fantastic worlds or invented cities? It will surely stimulate your creativity!

Take More Candid Pictures Exercise

Everyone, especially in today's world, seems to be obsessed with taking the perfect picture. There are some people who will post a single photo on social networks but have 100 more of the same position, background, and lighting stored on their phone. Still, the pictures are great for memories! They give you a physical remember of the place or situation you've been in. You have actual sights associated with the things that have happened in the past.

While you may already be taking pictures frequently, if you want to ensure that you have an efficient memory, then you should take the right kinds of pictures at the right time.

Photos are often taken with people lined up with their arms around each other and smiling. They'll find a picturesque background and wait until everyone is looking at the camera with their eyes open, smiling. These pictures are wonderful! However, many people forget to take more images besides these ones. While it's nice to have a photo of everyone together, it's also helpful to take real memories of smaller things just happening. We need to start ensuring that more candid pictures are taken. We need to take pictures of the moments and people around us that matter and capture them in the truest form that we can. Take photos without worrying about your flaws.

Pull out your camera and snap a photo as your friends are just sitting there. Take candid pictures of people serving their plates at a barbeque party. Capture images while everyone is in their pajamas, watching a movie. Take a picture of your friend as the two of you go for a nature walk. It doesn't matter what the situation is; just take more photos! These memories are unbeatable, for sure.

For this exercise, start taking a candid picture every day. Of course, be respectful of others and don't obnoxiously take a snap when you have no permission to do so. Still, every day for a week, pull out your phone and just take one candid shot. Don't focus on making it perfect. Pretend as though it's a disposable camera. Take one picture, and that's it! After a month, you will realize how many fond memories you have created. You may also see just how unique and memorable your experiences have been.

Reach Out

You might say, "How are you?" with the obligatory, "Good, how are you?" and then end it with "Good." on a daily basis. This is a common interaction among workers, coworkers, people on the street, and everyone else whom you just casually walk into. Change this up! You don't have to say the same thing day after day! Not everyone wants to discuss their lifestyle, but just change up the wording slightly or ask more specific questions. Open up the conversation if you want to! Here are some things that you can say instead of what's mentioned above.

- How are you feeling today?

- What's new with you?

- Has today been treating you nicely so far?

- Did anything surprise you today?

- How was today different than yesterday?

- Are you enjoying this lovely weather?

- Are you as tired as I am today?

- Who did you spend the most time with today?

- I hope your day has been interesting!

These are just examples. The more you socialize, the more you can remember things. Even when we're in a crowded room full of friends or relatives, it can be really easy to feel lonely. When you're not making those meaningful connections, you can get distracted and mentally remove yourself from the scenario. However, socializing and connecting to people — even in small ways — can help to keep you more aware of everything. This can improve your memory because you will be able to associate information with specific people and occasions.

Many people struggle with anxiety, so it isn't always peaches and cream when trying to reach out to others. If you are someone who gets sick to your stomach at the thought of even having to order a pizza over the phone, you are not alone. Take small steps. Don't force yourself into a situation that makes you uncomfortable. Start online and work your way up to talking to people in public. Socializing can be hard, but it's essential for increasing your brain power.

Puzzles

Puzzles are a great way to keep your brain active. Anytime you have to figure out how to get to a solution, you will be able to train your brain. Puzzles cause you to first look at the problem you have. What needs a solution from you? After that, you have to come up with a strategy to find it. If it doesn't work, then it's time to find a backup plan to get what you want. These are all incredibly important skills that can help us to fully embrace our cognitive abilities and increase our intelligence.

Crossword puzzle is a game that you should play. It stimulates the brain. The resolution involves reasoning and memory effort. It is always in newspapers, magazines, and other forms of paper media. Aside from that, you can go online and find crosswords. They may require trivia knowledge, but having general knowledge will be helpful as well.

Sudoku is another great game to try. It involves a 9-by-9 grid in which you have to fill in the boxes with any number between one to nine. Some people struggle with this puzzle because the numbers scare them away. They think that if they don't know how to do basic math, they won't be good at sudoku. There isn't math involved in the game, though, because there is no adding or subtracting. It's just a puzzle box where you have to supply the right symbol in the right spot. Start off with easy sudoku puzzles and work your way up to the expert puzzles. Alternatively, taking an empty sudoku grid and making your own puzzle can be equally as hard.

Word searches can keep your memory sharp. These things require little background knowledge whatsoever. It's a way for your brain to become trained in taking important and unimportant information and quickly differentiating between the two. A crossword puzzle forces you to look at letters and decide which ones are useful or can be ignored. This is a great way to keep your cognitive skills working overtime.

Jigsaw puzzles are also good for helping you to stay focused. They are often found in retirement homes for a reason! They keep our minds sharp and focused on logic. You have to look at the big picture of a jigsaw puzzle to understand where pieces really need to go. Then you should check a piece and decide if it is in the right spot. It taps into several parts of your brain and keeps you thinking logically. This is also excellent to do in group settings, as everyone loves being able to put a piece in!

Tetris is a popular game that can keep you mentally stimulated. It requires you to determine where the next piece will drop, you see. Games like this one on your pc, phone, tablet, or other device will allow you to stay sharp. There's no shame in playing a fun and colorful game! It doesn't mean that you are childlike; it's just that you are focused on increasing brain strength.

Staying on topic of fun and colorful games, I propose adult coloring books. Don't think this is just a hobby for children. They cause you to think creatively, but still within some restrictions so that your mind has something to focus on.

In addition to being a mental training, Art Therapy is also a creative method to reduce stress, promotes concentration and distracts you from negative thoughts.

It is now proven that coloring figures and drawings has anti-stress effects. This activity will also help you focus on the present moment, on the "here and now". So go back to coloring!

These brain games are just a few tools to increase your overall mental power.

Mental Yoga

Mental yoga is a practice to keep our stress levels down, oxygen flowing, and attention sharp. Traditional yoga is also good for your mental health, but not everyone has the physical strength to bend their bodies in crazy ways. Rather than trying to put your feet behind your head on the first day, therefore, you should begin with some mental yoga to give your brain clarity. Sometimes we believe that we have to always keep our minds running, pumping new information in. It's very important, however, to take time for our brains to rest. You should simply be able to sit there without allowing any thoughts in or out. This sounds easy, but you need some mind control. You have to close your eyes and look for the balance between body, mind, and spirit.

Having these moments when you simply thinking about nothing, gives your brain a chance to recharge. Giving yourself these moments of regeneration will help you live better and be happier. You will have greater awareness, strength of mind and physical and emotional well-being.

We may not think about how something small that happened in the morning can really affect the whole day. Instead, the early hours of the morning are the most important. Consider a time when you woke up super late for work. You might have stubbed your toe on the door running out, your hair was a mess so you're feeling self-conscious, and you had to skip breakfast yet again. You manage to make it through your day, but when you get home, you're still feeling grumpy and anxious. This is because your mind never had a moment to mentally clean itself from the emotions that you felt throughout the day. Everything you experienced affected your mood and emotions. You carried those thoughts throughout your day, and it could damage your ability to retrieve and store new information. Simple brain yoga exercises, however, helps cleanse you from the things that you should be forgetting so that you can focus on the most important aspects of your life.

Having a stress-free mind does not imply that you have eliminated all sources of stress in your life. It merely entails that you have learned how to manage that stress. When you can really take a moment to cool down from what you've experienced, it gives you all the power to get right back to what needs your utmost attention.

When you take care of your body and feel your health flourish inside you, you will be more focused on the things that matter most.

Find a place that will allow you to practice mental yoga. Outside on a calm patio or in a garden is a great place to start. When you can connect with nature, you can connect with your body. If it may not seem entirely possible, it's also fine to just do it inside the house. What's most important is that you are picking a spot that you can devote specifically to mental yoga exercises. If you do it in the same spot on the couch where you watch TV and binge sweets, this is where your mind will go. Pick a place that gives you complete mental clarity so that you don't have anything to focus on other than relaxing. This will also help because if you're having days where you don't feel your best and need that quick moment of relaxation, you can access that place and you will quickly find your state of well-being. It will become your safe space.

Somehow the places are real anchors that activate certain mental and emotional states. For example, I have a place for every kind of task I perform. This allows me to be much more productive and immediately enter the flow of productivity. Obviously, in addition to having places to recharge and regenerate myself.

To do mental yoga, choose a time when you feel most mentally exhausted to give your brain a chance to refresh and recharge. Finally, try to incorporate mental yoga with other forms of physical yoga as well. Exercising is good for you. These two methods will help you to stay mentally clear.

Pinky and Thumb

For this move, sit or stand up straight. Make sure that your spine is perfectly perpendicular to the floor. Focus on your breathing. Feel the air come into your body and leave it slowly. It's always good to start the exercises by breathing in and out through your nose.

Make a fist with both of your hands, but don't clench them incredibly tight. Keep them loose enough, just your fingers simply folded. Bring your fists up to your breast line and hold them there. Again, nothing should be too stiff. You don't want to create even more tension in the arms that you're trying to relax through these exercises.

With your right hand, stick your thumb out. All other fingers are tucked in your right hand, except for your thumb.

With your left, stick out your pinky. All other fingers on your left hand are tucked in besides your pink. Hold this pose for a moment while you continue to regulate your breathing.

On the count of three, switch how you're holding your hand. This means that you will go from holding the position we have just mentioned to sticking out your thumb on your left hand and your pinky on your right. While it sounds easy, it can be very challenging in reality. For the first try, you may find that all of your thumbs and pinkies are sticking out!

The point is to go from left pinky out, right thumb out, to left thumb out, right pinky out. Keep on practicing until you can make the switch in one swift movement with both hands at the same time. You will improve coordination.

Earlobe Hold

Start by breathing in deeply through your nose. Feel the air really come into your body and fill up your lungs. Let it out through your nose.

Take your right thumb and pointer finger and grab your left ear. Then, take your left hand and do the same with your right ear. Your arms should be in an X across your chest. Slowly, as you breathe in and out, let yourself fall into a squatting position.

Hold this for as long as you can. Repeat this process as needed. There is no trick with this one like the thumb-and-pinky exercise! It is simply a way to keep you focused on reducing stress and finding mental clarity.

Group Memorization Improvement Games

If you also want to improve the memory of your family or friends, know that playing group games is a great idea and will help you remember more.

If you're a teacher, camp leader, or someone who

loves working with others, then it's great to lead mindful activities among groups.

This helps you become a better leader as everyone will be focused on the same goal. Rather than creating competition among others, it can be great to keep them all together working towards a common goal.

Practice Fun Mindful Games Together

Like we mentioned earlier, it can be fun to do jigsaw puzzles together. Everyone will enjoy being able to find a puzzle piece. In addition to this, think of other puzzles that you can come up with.

How can you drop an egg from the top of the stairs without it breaking, for instance? What materials can you use to make a boat that will help to keep 10 pennies floating? How can you fit an egg into a bottle? Small activities like these seem so simple and like the things that we may do in elementary school. While it may be the case, they are also easy and virtually free ways to experiment in groups and have fun in building our cognitive abilities.

Eat Dinner Together

This is one of the best ways to be mindful. As you're eating dinner, take the time to share one new thing that you have learned that day. Don't wait until Thanksgiving to share what we are grateful for, do it as often as possible.

Another fun group activity is to discuss one good or bad thing that has taken place today. When you can come together and talk about substantial stuff like this, it can make your dinners much more meaningful.

Read Out Loud to One Another

This is a great way to work on your listening skills. You will have no pressure to respond and can simply focus on comprehending the words that are leaving someone else's mouth.

Go For a Walk and Point Things Out to Each Other

Listen to what others see and talk about your differing perspectives and what this can mean.

Play "I Spy"

I spy is a guessing game where one player chooses an object within sight and announces to the other players that "I spy with my little eye, something beginning with...", naming the first letter of the object. Other players attempt to guess this object.

It can also help you to discover more about the perspectives of those around you. What things do they see as important? Which parts around them stick out the most compared to what stands out to you?

Have intellectual discussions and give them a chance

to speak while you practice listening. After the game, keep talking and comparing. Don't just talk about what you did that day; mention your thoughts as well. What weird ideas did you have that you could discuss more? What strange daydreams did you imagine? What intellectual debate did you get into with yourself?

Here are a few other ideas for games that you can play in order to improve memory as a whole within a group.

Going on a Trip Game

This game will start with the idea that you and your group are going on a trip. Wherever the trip is doesn't matter a lot. You can play anywhere, sitting, standing, at home, or even while you are truly traveling. All you need is yourself and two or more other people.

The first person in the group will say something that they plan on bringing. You will want to envision a large suitcase or maybe someone's car trunk. You should name items you'd like to take with you on a trip.

The second person will add to that. Then, the third individual will add to that and so on. Each time someone goes, they will have to recite everything that has already been said.

The goal is to keep going to see how people will remember things. The first person to get the order wrong loses.

Here is an example of how this game may go:

Person 1: "I'm going on a trip, and I'm bringing underwear."

Person 2: "I'm going on a trip, and I'm bringing underwear and toothbrush."

Person 3: "I'm going on a trip, and I'm bringing underwear, toothbrush, and lotion."

Person 1: "I'm going on a trip, and I'm bringing underwear, toothbrush, lotion, and book."

Person 2: "I'm going on a trip, and I'm bringing underwear, toothbrush, lotion, book, and dress."

Person 3: "I'm going on a trip, and I'm bringing underwear, lotion, book, and dress."

As you can see, the last person would then lose because they forgot to say 'toothbrush.' The order is important, but you can decide within the group that it doesn't matter to you as long as they list all items correctly. If you are in a bar playing this game for your memory, you might decide that the loser offers coffee to everyone.

The ABC Game

This is a fun game to play when you're on a road trip. Sometimes time can go by so creakingly slow that you need to be engaged in a group activity for it to seem like it's not dragging on forever!

Start with 'A' and say something from any category that you want. You can do animals, foods, books, musicians, colors, and so on. The first person will state a word that starts with A, the second one will go with B and must be a word in the same category, the third person will do C, the fourth individual will mention something that starts with D, and so on. You don't have to repeat what others have said. You simply have to move down the letters of the alphabet.

Keep going. The first person to not think of anything is eliminated. If you can all agree within the group that there is nothing for a certain letter, such as "Books that start with X," then you can move on. There are a few books that start with X, but if everyone in the group is unaware of this, then you can move past it.

This game is really helpful because it forces you to logically navigate through your memory.

You're not just forced to recall things or items you've seen and heard of. You have to look for names that are specifically starting with one letter. You will still cycle through shows you know, but you will have to analytically pick one that fits the category and letter, calling from different parts of your brain at once and bringing them together.

The Game of Three Languages

As you know, my mother tongue is Italian. Years ago I happened to be at the beach and joined a group of multilingual boys and girls. There were Spanish and Latin Americans who only spoke Spanish, then there were English and Germans who spoke in English but not Spanish.

That day I found myself in the middle of being a translator. I listened in English, thought in Italian and spoke Spanish. I listened in Spanish, thought in Italian and spoke in English. Sometimes I happened to speak in Spanish when I had to speak in English and vice versa.

I have to say, that was really good mental training. Fortunately, I've had other times in my work speaking English and Spanish in the same conversation. Try creating a multilingual group of people and talking to them. Besides being a great workout, meeting people from other countries opens your mind.

3. Brain Power Exercises

Everything you are and do, involves your brain. From thought, to actions, from emotions to communicating with others. It is therefore clear that if you want to improve your life, you need to strengthen your brain.

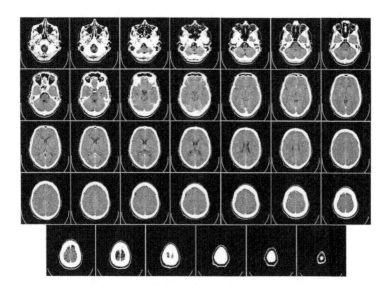

If you want to improve all aspects of your life, but

you don't take care of your brain, you won't make it. You also need to counteract the effects of the passage of time. So it is important to understand that the brain needs training. Training the brain means improving the performance of our life.

It's understandable if you do not feel like mentally working out. We all had those moments where we attempted a ninja move to grab the remote controller from a further distance instead of just getting up and walking to it. Don't let this happen again! Do not be lazy! Your brain will try to tell you to take the easy way out, because we are naturally built to conserve energy.

In the days when we had to live off the land, it was important to conserve even mental strength in case we had to fight off an enemy or if we couldn't find food for days at a time. Fight this urge to conserve too much because you can more easily replenish anything in our day and age.

Always look for ways to challenge your brain. Take each brain teaser as an opportunity to learn more and more. When something confuses you, try your best to discover more about it. Don't turn away just because something seems mentally confusing.

These are all exercises that will also help you in practical ways. Remember that these are activities to improve your brain and therefore your life.

Remember that your memory is just one part of your brain. If you want to really have a healthy memory, then strengthening everything else will be beneficial as well. Here are five exercises that will be fun to do, but actually workout your brain at the same time. These are the exercises that you don't need a gym membership for either!

Observe Things Backwards

Try doing this exercise. Take some photos, paintings, drawings, posters and start looking at them backwards. Put them underneath. Turn them upside down. Put them to the side. Observe these things in new ways. This technique allows you to create new points of view and create new perceptions, due to the fact that they will be new and unusual situations for your brain. You will create new connections and improve the integration between the two brain hemispheres.

But don't stop there. I want to encourage you to do something even more unusual. You can take some videos you have on your computer and then play them reverse with video editing software (there are many free ones too). Also play the audio of the video backwards. Or listen to your favorite song backwards. Or watch a video with the sound of another video.

These new, unusual stimulations will activate new areas of your brain. Learning to think outside the box is a good thing. You'll become more creative. Dare!

Math in Your Head

Performing some mental operations will help you to

increase your power of concentration and attention. Gradually increase the time you spend on these exercises. Your brain will get stronger. Let's begin.

One fun math exercise is to take a number — any number between one and ten — and multiply it by three. Then, multiply it by three again. Split the product in half and pick a number to divide it by in order to get as close as possible to the original number. This is just a quick way to get your brain thinking. So, remember that your number is X, and what you want to figure out is Y. Here is the equation: $3(3X) \div 2$. Then, with that answer, you will want to determine what you can divide it by to return to the original number.

Here's an example of how this would go if your number was 4.

$3 \times 4 = 12$

$12 \times 3 = 36$

$36 \div 2 = 18$

What can you divide 18 now by in order to get back

down to the original number of 4?

$$18 \div 4 = 4.5$$

$$18 \div 5 = 3.6$$

Is 3.6 closer to 4, or is 4.5 closer? The difference between 4 and 3.6 is 0.4, while subtracting 4.5 to 4 is 0.5. So, dividing 18 by 5 is your best option.

There's really not much of a point to this. As you can see, however, it takes you through multiple parts of a math problem. First, you have to fill in the numbers to be able to find your solution. But then, you need to look for other solutions as well and then pick out what digit works best. Not everyone thinks math is fun, but it's still an easy way to make you think and train your brain.

It's essential to keep up with our math skills. It goes beyond what one plus one means. We've gotten a little lazy with how we do math. Why bother when we have a calculator in our phones or computer, right? You will pretty much always have a calculator around, modern society is making you lose your computing skills. However, addition, subtraction, multiplication, division – all of these things are still very relevant to our lives.

In everyday life, always try to do the math in your head first. Then you can check your answer using a calculator. This is a little simple exercise that will help to keep your brain more energetic. It's like choosing the stairs over the escalator. You're still getting to the same place in the end, but at least you're training.

To really understand math, look at the numbers as a concept rather than a numerical digit or word. Two does not mean just '2.' Two means to have double of something. Think of dividing by four by figuring out what four parts are. Numbers are conceptual, not just stagnant digits. Create mental images to improve your understanding of things. You will improve your understanding of the world around you.

When you are leaving the tip at a restaurant, for instance, you should really be flexing your math skills. Somewhere in the world, a 10-year-old kid is doing calculus, so surely you can train your brain to understand how to tip without a calculator.

To determine how much you should tip, start by moving the decimal point to the left by one space. So, if your bill is $200.00, move the decimal to get $20.00. This is 10% of your total bill, which will always be the rule. Then, multiply it by what you want to tip. The standard is 10% to 20% or 25% if you're a great tipper! For a 15% tip, then you would take half of that 10% and add it to 10% to come up with $30. Half of $20 is $10, which equates to 5% of the total bill. 10% + 5% = 15%, so $20 + $10 = $30, which is equal to 15% of $200.00. For 20%, then you simply have to double 10%.

Think of this in terms of retail as well. A dress is listed at $56, and the discount is 40%. What is 10% of the dress? $5.60. You want to know what 40% is, though, so you will take $5.60 and multiply it by 4. This may be hard to do in your head first, so start by multiplying $5 by 4, which would be $20. Then, you have $0.60 multiplied by 4. Multiplying decimals can be scary, but just pretend as if there's no decimal there. You will then have 60 x 4 = 240. That is equivalent to 240 cents, which is $2.40. Add this to $20 to get a total of a $22.40 discount. Subtract the number from $56, and you can have the dress for $33.60.

This all sounds complicated, but it is an example of how you can quickly break things down into the smallest parts to get the actual answer that you're looking for.

Look for tricks to remember more challenging multiplication formulas as well. For example, if you take 6 and multiply it by any even number, then the last digit of that will be the same as the number in which you multiplied it. See for yourself:

6 x $\underline{2}$ = 1$\underline{2}$

6 x $\underline{4}$ = 2$\underline{4}$

6 x $\underline{6}$ = 3$\underline{6}$

6 x $\underline{8}$ = 4$\underline{8}$

6 x 10 = 60

6 x 12 = 72

6 x 14 = 84

6 x 16 = 96

You get the point. There are other tricks like this in order to help you remember your multiplication tables.

You can use your hands to determine what things can be multiplied by 9. What you will want to do is take your left and right hands and hold them out in front of you, palms towards you. Now, from your left thumb to your right pinky, they represent numbers 1 to 10. So, on your left hand, you have your thumb (1), pointer finger (2), middle finger (3), ring finger (4), and pinky (5). Then, on your right hand, you have your pinky (6), ring finger (7), middle finger (8), pointer finger (9), and thumb (10).

For multiplying digits by 9, look at which number you will be multiplying. This number then represents which finger you will fold down. Then, the number on the left side of the folded down finger is the first digit to your answer, while the number of fingers on the other side is the right side of the digit.

For example, let's do 9 x 3. You would fold down your middle finger on your left hand. This leaves you with two fingers on the right side (left thumb/left pointer finger) and then seven fingers on the other side (left index finger/left pinky/all five right fingers). So, the first number would be 2 and the second number would 7. It will then give you 27.

These are just a few mathematical activities that you can do when you have the chance. Always look for ways to challenge yourself. It can be easy to reach for that calculator but try to do the math in your head first.

Fast Reading Exercise

I don't want to talk to you about quick reading techniques, I want to talk to you about an exercise. Open a book at random from your bookstore, open it in the middle and start reading a page very quickly. Read as fast as you can trying to get the meaning of the speech. Try to remember everything you read. How many parts have you forgotten? Why did you remember those sentences and not others? Practice. It's good mental stimulation.

Learning How to Cook

Knowing how to cook is a valuable skill that we should all develop, but it should not just be for our stomach's sake. The foods that you choose to eat will directly affect how your brain works. You are what you eat because it will become a part of you!

Cooking at home is better for your health, especially because you will know what is in every dish. Fast food and prepackaged meals can be tempting to reach for initially because they're so easy to consume. However, remember that you still have to give your brain power foods!

In this exercise you won't have to focus on learning

how to memorize recipes. But you will need to stimulate your thinking to understand how something is made and why certain ingredients work. This will allow you to discover your love of cooking.

Learn the different ways to cook chicken. You may read a recipe that calls for 2 tablespoons of olive oil, 2 tablespoons of lemon, 1 clove of garlic, salt, and pepper to taste. Do you know why these ingredients have been chosen? What can you add to make it even better? Will rosemary work here? What about adding sage? When you can understand how something actually works from the core, it becomes easier to experiment with it.

How is seafood prepared best? Did you know that you can cook it in the oven, on the stove or grill, and even in the fridge by keeping it soaked in an acid-like lemon juice?

Think about the recipes you read, try to understand the processes, think about what you can change and why, also you can change them based on what ingredients you may already have. Furthermore, you may omit things so that the dish can cater to your personal taste.

If you are already someone who knows how to cook, it'll be a lot easier. It's a great skill to have, after all. Why don't you try teaching it to others as well? Create a cookbook that you can pass down to different friends and family members.

In addition to this, you should learn how to garden and keep fresh vegetables if your environment permits. Gardening is a great way to tap into all five of your senses. Aside from that, it is a source of accomplishment that will make you feel good about yourself.

The reason why cooking is beneficial is that it helps us use executive functions within our brains. Some things help us keep our focus, come up with our next plan of action, stick to goals, and use memories to apply logic (Cleveland Clinic, 2017).

When you cook a meal, you are planning, preparing, organizing, multitasking, and reflecting. You take your brain through multiple layers of thinking, helping it to work itself out while also doing something practical and beneficial to your life.

Not many tasks can do all of this at once. Cooking consumes all your focus while working out different parts of your brain. The best part of all is that there will be a literal reward at the end: the delicious meal that you get to enjoy!

Imagine Tastes and Smells

Sight is the dominant and most important sense, but

taste and smell are also very powerful. These two senses are very effective in stimulating memory. How many times have you experienced a taste or smell that you haven't felt in a long time, and in that moment your mind begins to relive emotions from the past. This is because tastes and smells are able to activate an instant emotional reaction in us.

These two senses have a special and direct connection with the hippocampus which is the seat of memory that allows us to store information and emotions.

Having said that, in relation to the previous exercise, you can sit comfortably on the sofa or an armchair and imagine preparing a recipe. Try to imagine all the smells of fresh ingredients, then the preparation phase and finally the smell of the finished dish.

Don't stop at recipes, also try to remember the best moments of your life. Relive those emotions evoking tastes and smells from the great archive of your memory.

Memories of the Past

This exercise can also be linked to the previous one. You can relive memories of the past that are particularly exciting for you. Think of people, events, happenings that really moved you. Your first love, your first kiss, a nice evening with friends, a business success, graduation, the birth of a child, your best friend's wedding or your son's first day at school.

What I'm about to propose is that you go up to the attic of your grandparents' house and get everything out of the memory boxes. Games, greeting cards, black and white and colour photos, gifts received and objects from your old room.

Of course you don't necessarily have to have a real attic, but I hope I've helped you better understand the exercise.

Remember your experiences. Relive those emotions. In doing so, you will stimulate your concentration, creativity and many other areas of your memory, in short, you will activate your mind completely. While nice, remember not to get stuck in the past. The present is the only thing we have. You have to live it to the fullest. Carpe diem.

Imagine a Future Scene

Still in the wake of previous exercises, try to start imagining a scene of tomorrow's day. Such as your lunch. Start by looking at the details of the table and chairs. How is the table set? How many objects are there? Think about the food now. Start identifying yourself until you really feel the taste and smell of your lunch. Stimulate your sensory perceptions, try to take advantage of all five senses. Now focus on your hearing. What do you hear? Listen to the sounds of your cutlery and dishes. What other sounds can you hear?

The Unusual Object

With this exercise I still want you to use your imagination and stimulate your creative thinking.

Think of the common objects. Imagine taking them and using them for something. Like a hammer, a shovel or a wooden ladle.

Just don't imagine you using them in the traditional way. Try to imagine a completely different creative use. Like for example mixing a rice with a hammer. Let your imagination run wild.

Now I want to propose another variation of this exercise. Locate an object and think about what other use you could make of it. For example, imagine a balloon, or pick one up. Look at it carefully.

What other use can you make of it? Did it ever occur to you that you might split it in two? You could take a part and make four equidistant holes in the edge. Then run a rope through the holes and hang it under a porch to make a pot of plants suspended in the air.

Or think about your waste materials. Like a can or a glass bottle. In what different context could you reuse these objects?

Playing an Instruments

Many people can play an instrument without thought, but others don't understand music at all. Whether you are a musical child prodigy or someone who's never even strummed a guitar, it's still important to include playing an instrument as a part of your life to strengthen your memory and other cognitive functions.

If you already know an instrument, then that's much better. You can choose to practice it further or pick up another one. If you have other musician friends, then consider swapping instruments for a month, giving each other a lesson, or doing something else to share this experience.

Pick a musical instrument that you actually want to learn how to play. If money is an issue, then you may even consider playing a virtual synthesizer through your tablet. Play with free music apps. It's not always a requirement to know how to read music either. You can simply start to play around by plucking some strings and pressing some buttons. Get carried away, think of nothing and let your imagination run wild.

There are many reasons why playing an instrument can be beneficial to your mental health. There are so many of them. You'll have psychological, cognitive and social benefits.

First, it teaches you responsibility. It gives you a valuable skill and helps you to learn more about yourself. Playing improves your cognitive skills, makes your brain more responsive to sensory stimuli and prevents brain aging. It helps you stay alert, active and lucid. But you'll also improve your organizational skills because playing an instrument also means learning how to manage your time.

Your mathematical skills and calculating skills will also improve. Because playing also stimulates your mathematical logical reasoning skills. Those who can read a score also have a greater ability in seed reading and text comprehension. And you won't believe this, but it is now proven that playing an instrument makes us smarter because playing it increases our IQ.

But now let's talk about the social aspects. Music promotes socialization. It allows you to socialize because you will meet other people with the same passion as you. Shall we talk about the advantages of having a band? I've had many in the past. Somehow it forces you to perform in public and it's a great way to beat shyness. Performance after performance, you will become more confident. Not to mention that playing together with a band teaches you how to work together to achieve a common goal. Music promotes socialization and harmony with others.

Of course, playing a musical instrument is a great way to use your memory. You will use your memory and your reasoning skills at the same time. You'll need to extract information from what you already know and think about what you can do to improve your skills or how you should adjust so that you can produce the best possible sound.

So start playing an instrument, it will also help reduce stress. You can dedicate a time every day to work on your instrument, ensuring that you're focused on improving yourself and relaxing. It is a way to feel like you have accomplished something and then feel better about yourself.

Just like with cooking, you are also developing your patience. You accept that you won't become Mozart overnight. It will require some patience and reflecting to become the best musician possible at the time.

Playing any instrument will keep both sides of your brain working as well. It takes the creative, analytical, logical, and reasoning parts and then combines all of them together.

Dear reader, now you'll have to forgive me if I don't finish this paragraph without a bit of publicity first. Music has always been a great passion of mine, and I've been writing melodies and songs since 1997. Some of them come from my guitar, others from the piano, others from the computer thanks to virtual instruments.

My stage name has always been Eddie Lover. If you want, visit my website (eddielover.com) and subscribe to my social channels, especially on Youtube. I would love to share with you my past, present and future creations.

Drawing from Memory

For this memory exercise, you will have to choose a medium to work with. Whether it's a canvas to paint with brushes, oil paints, watercolours, charcoals or pencils and sketchbook, choose something that you will feel most comfortable using.

Next, pick a place that you are going to recreate. This can be a corner in your house or a beautiful Tuscan hill. Whatever you choose, work with what you see. The next step is to recreate it from your memory. Take your time to study the area without writing notes. Close your eyes, imprint the image in your mind and start thinking about how you're going to draw it. Imagine the process, open your eyes and start drawing.

If you really want to challenge yourself, pick a spot that you haven't seen in a while. Maybe you went to New York City as a child, and the skyline inspired you. Can you draw this from memory?

Try to recreate the exact image in your mind and try to get every detail correctly. Even if it's wrong, figure out how you can fill in the space you can't remember with something else. You don't have to draw it in the same way either, stick with what you know! You can draw it in a cartoon style or maybe color stuff using only three different shades of your choice.

Pick scenes and pictures online if you want as well.

Just look at the image for some time as you will do with a regular scene and then don't look at it anymore.

The point is to teach yourself how to notice what you may remember the most. Is the big detail the easiest for you to recall? Or do you pay more attention to the smaller details? Repeat this activity on a regular basis. It's similar to drawing a map; however, instead of the overall picture, you're focused on the small details. To fill in the spaces and actually recreate the images that you've seen, you should compare them with the originals and reflect on what you have done correctly and incorrectly.

This activity will teach you a lot about your own mind. You might discover that you completely forgot something or that you might have a better photographic memory than you give yourself credit for.

Anyway, to improve your photographic memory, remember that the first book in this series: *"Photographic Memory"*, will help you.

Imagine if you are in a certain place, how will you draw it? What points would you focus on the most? This is an activity that stimulates the brain, besides improving your memory, it will also improve your creative abilities. Another aspect not to be underestimated, thanks to this technique, you will be able to capture more of the small details that surround you and you will become an excellent observer.

What Is It?

This is a simple exercise and also fun that you can do with your friends. Select a couple of objects each without showing them to the others and then in turn, blindfolded, you should recognize the objects, just relying on your touch. Then touch it with your hand.

You will begin to dig into your memory your previous experiences, creating comparisons and similarities. Will you be able to recognize objects with your eyes closed?

Laughter in company is guaranteed! Go back to playing with your friends, it's good for life!

Playing Brain Games

I don't know if you're a person who likes to play games on your computer or your smartphone. Personally, I don't really like smartphones. My main phone is a very common phone without touchscreen. But if you're someone who uses it a lot, then why don't you combine the useful with the enjoyable and play mini-games that are fun and improve your mental skills at the same time?

Anyway, I suggest you use the computer to do these mental workouts. I'll give you a wide choice of different types, so I'm sure you'll find something to your liking. Remember, you can find other games on **upgradeyourmemory.com**.

When choosing a game to play, you want to pick one that is most comfortable for your brain. What do you like to do the most? Do you enjoy more exciting word games? Is it with puzzles that you feel the most comfortable with? You like mental calculus better?

Of course, this is just a book and not an interactive app, so I'm going to suggest a few great software and websites that will expand your mind.

Explore all of your options and always look for ways to try new and fun games.

Mindgames

Mindgames.com is a good website full of games. They have so many games, so you will never get sick of playing the same thing twice. Maybe you're someone who spends hours every day on social media, online shops, and other things on your computer.

Keep this bookmarked and just play for 10 minutes daily.

Lumosity

Lumosity is backed by some experts and can help to keep you focused on improving specific parts of your brain. You can use the app and get games that are specific to the parts of your brain that you need to work on the most.

The program promises to help you improve memory, attention, flexibility, processing speed and troubleshooting.

Braingle

Braingle.com is a fun source of brain teasers. This is an example of a mind game from the website:

"Take the given words, and by moving a single letter from one word to the other, make a pair of synonyms, or near synonyms. For example, with the given Boast - Hip, move the 's' from 'Boast' to 'Hip' to create two synonyms, Boat - Ship."

Rode - Can

Font - Farce

Tory - Stale

Dire - Cash

Self - Shill"

The answer?

"1. Rod - Cane

2. Front - Face

3. Story - Tale

4. Die - Crash

5. Shelf - Sill"

Brain games should become a regular part of your life. Train as hard as you can.

Brain Challenge 2.0

This is a very popular game produced by Gameloft and is available on console, computer and mobile. There are 20 exercises divided into 5 categories: Memory, Logic, Mathematics, Vision and Focus. You can test yourself by setting different levels of difficulty. You will find exercises for the stimulation of mnemonic skills, for improving reflection and deduction, for your arithmetic calculation skills, for your ability to quickly intuition in front of images and for your attention and concentration skills.

Memocamp

Memocamp.com can be considered a real gym for your mind. It is a portal that provides different methods with which you can test your memory, train it and even monitor your progress. You will be pleased to know that most people who participate in world memory competitions train on this portal. You can train for free with the first levels, after which you will need the paid version.

Memoriad

Memoriad is a great mental sports competition held every 4 years, since 2008, in a different international city. It can be defined as the Olympic Games of Mind. On memoriad.com you can download free software where you can train your mind through various exercises. The main categories are: Memory, Mental Calculation and Photographic Reading.

Speed Memory

Speed Memory - created by the multiple world champion of fast memory Ramón Campayo - is both a training system and a competition. This software helps you develop strength and mental speed and is the official Speed Memory competition program. The spectacular speed at which the tests are carried out minimizes the difference between participants and fills the competition with emotion.

You can download the software for free at

speed-memory.com, it will help you to improve your concentration and attention, you will learn how to store things in no time and you will develop your photographic memory. You can train even a few minutes a day, but the results are guaranteed.

Remember that on **upgradeyourmemory.com** you will find not only other virtual games but also physical games to train your mind. Save it among your favorites, the site will be continuously updated with the best news.

Neurobics and Neurobic Exercises

Neurobics is the fusion of the words "neurons" and "aerobics", this term was coined by Lawrence C. Katz and Manning Rubin. Neurobics is a discipline that helps keep your brain in shape. It helps you to create new connections between neurons, and this is important to improve your brain's functions. To keep your brain young in addition to keeping the synapses you have active, which is a junction between two neurons, you need to create others. So you have to create new neural connections, you have to form new connections between neurons. Although the number is not always important, but the efficiency.

Cognitive decline occurs due to the reduction in the complexity, number and efficiency of dendrites. Dendrites are the minor fibres that branch out from the neuron. Doing the same thing over and over for years and years makes dendrites atrophy.

The connections between dendrites are called synapses. If there are not enough connections or these connections do not take place on a regular basis, dendrites can atrophy. The lack of novelty weakens the brain. It turns off your creativity, and your ability to adapt. This atrophies the brain.

Unfortunately, the fake comforts of modern society help you to use your brain less and less. The comforts lazy your mind. And you don't have to fall into the usual habits, although there are some good habits you have to maintain, there are many others that slowly turn off your brain.

So, what do you do to revitalize your mind and not fall into the usual routine? You have to use your senses in a new way. You need to be more curious, learn new things, be open to change and have an active social life. In short, more emotions and stimulating situations. You need to stimulate your brain through new experiences that involve your senses and emotions.

All this will help you to enhance synapses between neurons, regrow dendrites and stimulate the production of neurotrophins, a family of proteins that determine the survival, development and function of neurons.

You need to know that neurons don't only develop in children's brains, they also develop in adults' brains. Even older neurons can develop. That's when neurobics come to our aid, helping us to make neural cells stronger and more resistant to ageing. So here we are helped by the neurobics, which helps us make neural cells stronger and resistant to aging.

Neurobic exercises will stimulate you to face new experiences, improve memory loss and prevent your brain from deteriorating even more.

These exercises are based on breaking the routine, changing the patterns that have set in your mind, training your brain to deal with new situations and then make it more elastic in adapting to changes. Are you ready to improve your mental elasticity now?

Perform neurobic exercises as many times as you can. Change them often and always bring new variations, because doing the same things every day will eventually make them ineffective. Then, you can go back to the way that you used to do things as well.

Get Dressed in the Dark

This activity can help you to use your brain to figure

out how to put on clothes without using your eyes. Of course, ensure that you won't hurt yourself while doing so.

Shower With Your Eyes Closed

Wash your body with your eyes closed and feel your body parts that need washing rather than looking at yourself. As mentioned above, try to do it without harming yourself.

These two exercises allow you to look for an alternative strategy to achieve the result without using your sense of sight. This will help you stimulate the sense of touch, which of the 5 senses, is often the most asleep.

Swap What You Do in the Morning and at Night

Maybe you wake up everyday at 7 am to work out and then read for an hour before work. Then, at night, perhaps you take a walk and do the laundry before heading to bed. Well, for a change, try to switch such activities! Do the opposite and alter your routine even if the change is minimal.

Switch the Hand That You Use for an Entire Day

If you are right-handed, switch the hand that you brush your teeth with. Wear your watch on the opposite wrist. Change the hand that you use to pour water into a glass as well. Alter the hand that holds the dishes and sponge.

Try even writing with the other hand if you can! Of course, don't do this in a professional setting, but this is really good exercise that help to work out your brain.

Change Your Way of Eating

If you always devour your meal at the kitchen

counter, eat it on the dining table instead. f you eat with your family, change the order of seats at the table.

Try different restaurants as well. Don't just go to the same place and order the same thing off the menu. Get something weird and try foods that you never would have consumed otherwise.

This idea can make some people nervous. They're afraid to take something they don't like and leave everything on their plate. Next time you go out to eat with other friends, get some dishes to share. This way, you will have things you can try, but you won't run the risk of not eating anything.

Why don't you invite someone you don't know to lunch? You always learn something new.

Test your memory, recreate the lunch from when you went to eat at your grandparents' house or the recipes from your wedding lunch. It will be fun and exciting.

Make Changes in Your Office

Every now and then, make changes in your work environment. You could change the position of the knick-knacks, move your computer and pen holder. Always make changes.

Watch TV or Listen to a Song That You Dislike

I hardly ever watch TV. But we often watch things that we only want to see. For a change, tune in to a TV show that you would never want to watch or pick out a movie that you've been avoiding for a while now. Even though you may still not enjoy watching it, you can learn something new and stimulate new points of view.

Listen to a Song That You Dislike

Choose a genre of music you don't like, and then listen to a song. It could be a source of growth. It can introduce you to something you didn't know, you can get to know realities unknown to you. Think of a popular song from a different country that can convey culture and traditions. Or for example a trap song that could give us some food for thought to better understand the realities of young people who follow that style of music.

Music has always been an important instrument of culture and information. Few people pay attention to the hidden messages that are hidden in songs. You will find a lot of important information in songs that you don't like.

Sit at the Opposite End of Your Couch

We all have our favorite sitting spot at home. Rather than going straight for the same place, though, choose something different today.

Switch Up The Scents in Your Home

Lavender and vanilla may be your top scents, but don't hesitate to try a new fragrance. You can always go back to what you like, but it's nice to switch up the scents for your brain.

Change Your Journey to Work in the Morning

It doesn't matter if you go to work by car, public transport, or go walking. Tomorrow, take the long way that's more scenic for once.

Change the Grocery Store That You Always Go to

You know your grocery store so well that you shop automatically without activating your brain. Tomorrow go shopping in a place you've never been before.

Listen to Karaoke Versions of Songs When

You Plan on Singing

Whether you're in the shower or car, choose the version without words so that you can figure out how to keep up with the rhythm and say the right words better.

Try New Sports

Trying new sports is very good for you, you will train and stimulate your motor and coordination skills in a different way. You will also become stronger in your main sport.

Try New Hobbies

Try new hobbies to stimulate your creativity. Sign up for some short courses in drawing, painting, ceramic, sculpture or photography. You will feel like a much more complete person.

Communicate More With Others

Even if silence and moments of solitude are good for you, invent opportunities to have a chat with new people. Go into a small local shop and exchange a few words with the shopkeeper. Maybe while you're on the plane or train exchange a few opinions with your local neighbor.

Change Your Holiday Experience

Always change your holiday destinations. Try new experiences. Visit new cities and countries. Dedicated to activities you've never tried before. Alternatively spend your holidays in a hotel, at home or camping. And wherever you go, pay attention to the diversity of colours, sounds and scents of different places.

Other Changes

Alternate the background on your phone. Rearrange

your furniture. If you always wear a watch, you go out without it. If you don't wear it, wear it for a day. Always look for ways to do things differently from what you're already doing. You want to make the most of it? Go live for rent and move house every year. It will be a storm of new stimuli and emotions, in every sense. (Obviously you have to make the houses you own profitable, but I won't talk business here like I do with *Zeloni Corporation* → _zeloni.eu_).

4. Memorization Techniques

We all have things that need to be remembered. While it's important for your quality of life to hold on to good memories and learn from the bad, we also still have to learn new information and memorize them.

When we were kids and went to school, we learned many things by heart, but we only did to get good grades. But that's not what you have to do anymore. You have to memorize information so you can understand the things around you better.

There are ways to improve your memorization skills. They are practical tricks, such as card games, as well as common techniques that will help you to improve how you memorize new information.

Make Sure That You Are in a Study-Safe Place

Libraries and literary cafés can work great because others around you will be studying as well. There will be an overall focused vibe that can work better for you than the common areas in your home where your relatives may disturb you. Unless you have a perfect place that encourages study and learning.

Remove All Distractions

This way, you only have to focus on the most important bits of information. Forget about watching TV at the same time, leave the phone in another room. Focus only on studying.

Write Things Down

Even if you're watching an instructional video, writing things down is important. On one hand, it provides a reference you can go back to later. On the other, it helps you to remember what information you're learning about. If you have already read the first book of this series *"Photographic Memory"* I invite you to reread chapter 6 on Mind Mapping. Don't just take boring monochrome notes. Learn how to use the power of mind maps.

Repeat Words Out Loud

When you can verbally say things, it sticks in your brain more easily than if you just listen to it. Also try to imagine a classroom full of people to whom you have to tell what you studied. Talk to them.

Actively Repeat Yourself

Learning about something once doesn't mean that you already know everything. Go back and test what you know.

Reflective Reading

I often use my "Reflective Reading" method. I take a few sentences from a book that express a concept, and I go for a walk for a couple of hours and always reflect on those same words. What did the author really want to tell us? What is the real meaning of those sentences? Believe me, most people don't really understand the meaning of many sentences. There are books that I reread and reread them over and over again. And the more I reread them, the more I understand the real message the author wanted to convey. If you study with this method of mine, you will truly understand the true meaning of the sentences and you will indelibly tattoo in your mind the concepts that really make a difference in a person's life.

Test yourself as Often as Possible

Thinking you know doesn't always mean you really know something. Socrates was right all along. The only true wisdom is in knowing you know nothing.

Even if you've already taken an advanced course on

that subject, never stop studying it. There will be other videos and resources that can still help you learn more about that particular subject. Studying from multiple sources gives you a more complete view of things. Of course, you have to be good at selecting the right sources. It may seem easy, but it's not.

Card Games

Cards can allow you to implement new learning techniques in your life.

We all have a deck of cards lying around. Why not use it to train your brain? There are plenty of fun packs as well aside from the standard four-suit, four-color cards.

Flash cards are a great way for you to memorize things, for example. Create them with a structure that allows them to be flipped over easily. They are widely used for study and storage, and you can even make them yourself with a simple Bristol board.

There are various ways you can use flashcards. There are various ways you can use flash cards. You could for example write questions on one side and answers on the other. Or you could draw pictures on the front and words on the back. Also try writing a keyword on side 1 and a broad description of what you need to remember on side 2.

Now back to our deck of cards. Before we teach you how to memorize a pack of cards, there are a few other short games that you can play. The first one is identifying the color, number, and suit of a deck of cards.

Go through the deck and take out the cards one by one. For each card that you pull out, you should say the color, number, and suit out loud. So, if it's a five of hearts, you have to say, "Red, five, hearts". You have to say it as fast as you can to improve your reaction time. Do this for each card until you make it to the end. That's it! That's the game! While it's not as riveting as others, it still helps you to add verbal cues to physical objects and literal imagery. It will help you improve your reflexes.

The next activity will switch things up a bit.

- Start in the same with a full deck of cards.

- Say only the number for the first card

- Pronounce only the colour for the second card

- Pronounce only the suit for the third card

- Until the end of the deck alternates number, color and suit.

This is just as simple as the first; only, it causes you to think a little more. Always remember to be as fast as possible. You can keep the deck of cards with you at all times and pull them out whenever you need to exercise your brain just a bit.

How to Memorize a Pack of Cards

Why would you want to memorize a deck of cards, you might ask?

Once you learn how to memorize information in that form, it will become easier to memorize bigger chunks of information. It's not the actual deck of cards that you're worried about; instead, it's how you practice memorizing other important details.

Memorize information in a certain order is important because it can help you remember anything once you've mastered this skill.

The first thing you will want to do is to break the

cards down into smaller groups. There are 52 cards in one deck Start with a quarter of that, which will mean 13 cards. Start even smaller if you want with groups of five and then one final group of just two. Go as small as you want and break up the card into these piles.

After this, it is then time to run through the deck once. Give yourself a briefing. What cards exist within each pile? Don't worry about memorizing them in this moment as much; just focus on what cards are in which pile.

Now, you want to find an association for each card. What does the number 2 mean to you? What about a red heart? When you can latch these suits and numbers to a physical image, then you will be able to remember the cards better.

Then, start to memorize one pile at a time. Recall them individually and then add them altogether. You might end up discovering that you can also memorize the complete deck right away. Our brains are all different, but this method of grouping is usually best for beginners.

From there, make your stacks bigger and bigger. Break it down into just two different piles and memorize the cards again. Eventually, you'll be able to do the entire stack at once with ease.

The key here is to group the cards into smaller bits and then find ways to associate them with the things that you already know. For example, your deck has:

- Five of hearts
- King of spades
- Five of diamonds
- Queen of hearts
- Jack of spades

Five of hearts is equal to **family** because you have five family members who all have hearts. King of spades equates to a **gardener** because a king, who is a master of spades, is like a gardener. Five of diamonds can mean **rich** because having five diamonds means that you probably have a lot of money. Queen of hearts can be **Alice** because of the character in *Alice in Wonderland*. Jack of spades may then be **trades** because it sounds like the jack of all trades. Each card now has a completely unique association due to what you remember most. The order then becomes:

- Family

- Gardener

- Rich

- Alice

- Trades

You can use these words to even create a quick story.

Maybe it's something like, "My family gardener is rich because his daughter, Alice trades." It doesn't make any sense, but it doesn't always have to! It simply becomes easier to remember these small word-associated signals. Therefore, you have a better chance to recall the card orders later on.

Eventually, this skill will help you to memorize numbers, names of groups of people, and other things that may come to you in bulk.

Memory Matching Game

An easy card game that can allow you to improve your memory is the matching game. You can do this with a deck of cards, as well as other cards that come in pairs.

For a deck of cards, link things based on number and color. There are four kings in a deck but only two red kings.

Lay the cards out in a grid. So you'll have horizontal rows and vertical rows. It should be an organized grid that's based on the number of cards that you have in the entire deck.

If you're going alone, pick up two at once. If you're playing with others, take turns picking up two at once. The aim of the game is to take two identical cards (for example, the two red kings).

If they're right, remove the cards from the grid. The person with the most matches in the end wins. It's a really easy game that pulls your memorization skills to the forefront. It gives you the opportunity to keep in mind what you have just seen. Memory matching game is easy to play with children as well.

Visualization, Associations and Method of Loci

The visualization is very effective for a better memory. This is because most of our cerebral cortex is dedicated to visual information processes. Thinking in images will make your memories more understandable and effective.

Suppose you're studying for a test. You can look at the room in front of you and associate one word with one object. Each time you have to learn something new, think of it along with a physical object that you see. When the time comes for you to take the test, you can image travel back through the room where you were studying and pick up each object, remembering the information that you have associated with it along the way.

This technique is important because our human brains won't always remember facts and things so easily. We are more likely to envision an entire situation when trying to recall something. It's easier to tell a story that you experienced rather than say something that you only read about. After all, we receive and process a lot of information simultaneously.

Tell a story with what you are memorizing. It'll be a lot easier to remember. In your stories there must be action and emotional content, this will allow you to create something relevant for your brain and therefore easy to remember.

Some of the things you imagine may be crazy. Perhaps you think of yourself and your family running down a mountain with snow everywhere, a hippo in a tuxedo, an elephant in a bathing suit, and five tap-dancing cats. Whatever you are visualizing, though, just go with it!

Let logic go at the moment. All that matters is that you're associating real information with an image that helps to keep it stored in your brain.

A common way to link information is the method of loci, also used by the ancient Romans. This is when you are able to associate a familiar place with information that you're trying to remember. You can use the idea of a path throughout this location to remember things in order. For instance, imagine walking through your home. The toaster on the right reminds you of the first step of the process of photosynthesis. Then, there's the microwave on the left that you associated with the second. There's also the stove, fridge, and door leading to the hallway. Each thing that sticks out in your mind will remind you of one of the important steps that you're trying to remember. What's important is that you can connect something new with what you already are familiar with.

Have a Memory Token

Keep a small penny or stone in your pocket. When you have to remember something, touch the stone. Then, when you need to recall that information later, you can touch it again. At the end of the day, when you're filling out your calendar for tomorrow, you can touch the stone and think to yourself, "When else have I touched this today? What did I need to remember?"

Associate new information with all five senses as quickly as you can One of the greatest ways to improve your memory or remember a setting in general is by stimulating all five senses. E.g., your sight, hearing, touch, smell, and taste.

Let's say that you meet someone, a new girl named Tamara. When she says, "Hi, I'm Tamara", associate it with your five senses. Think of something like, "Tamara smells like a rose. She looks like my neighbor. Her hands are hot and dry. She has a very sweet voice. My mouth tasted like coffee when we met." This will help you remember her better, as well as the time of your meeting.

Create a Song

What you can also do is create a song. Some people recall things more easily when they can turn them into a fun song. The trick is to use a song that you already know. Replace the original lyrics with words that you are trying to remember.

Testing Your Memory

We should all try our best to check in with our memory. You may do many activities for a few weeks and then stop because you notice an improvement. Eventually, if you stop working out your brain, you'll lose the benefits. You have to exercise it constantly if you want long-term results. It affects your quality of life. Occasionally, do some tests to monitor yourself.

Trivia is a great technique to test your memory. Even though you may not have the expert knowledge, such as info from science or movie categories, you can still use trivia as a way to test your ability of using context clues.

Tell stories with great detail, too. Write your own books about your own experiences! When you can create detailed visuals along with what your experiences, it becomes much easier to recall important information.

Aside from doing these things, there is a simple memory test that you can include in your life. Let's do it now, it's very quick.

Look at the chart below and remember as many words as you can. Give yourself 30 seconds and then look away. Start when you're ready.

Barn	Square	Compass	Stethoscope
Radio	Pencil	Doctor	Helicopter
Snake	Candle	Brush	Toilet

Now, list out as many of these twelve words as possible. How many correct answers did you get?

- Getting 10 or 12 shows that you have a good short-term memory.

- Getting between 6 and 9 means you're doing okay.

- Getting less than 6 shows that you need some serious memory training.

This is a really simple test. They're in a random order in the chart, but it doesn't mean that you have to remember them in the same way. Create other tests similar to this one, have a friend choose the words and check your memory status. Look for other ways to always check in with your own mind

(Cherry, 2019).

5. Mastering New Activities

When you have a trained memory and your cognitive skills are functioning properly, then you may realize how easy it is to learn new things. However, there are still other methods to learn new information more effectively.

Keep in mind that not every skill you learn has to be repeated on a regular basis. Sometimes we just have to learn something new temporarily, such as a small procedure at work that you will only be doing for a couple months. Whatever it is, it's still important to understand it at its core.

Whether you want to memorize someone's name quickly or pick up the rules of a new game, there are a few things you can do to learn new information easily. For one, don't be intimidated by the things that you don't know. There are many people in the world who get incredibly frustrated when they don't understand something. This often occurs because they feel insecure about their level of intelligence. However, you should never feel bad about yourself even if you're not picking things up as easily as others may do.

Start convincing yourself you can learn anything, and you will. The limits exist only in your mind. It's your beliefs about what you can do that limit you.

Push yourself harder than what your up-level may

do. Try to improve your mental strength. Here's a way to do it. If you have to do a task in an hour, challenge yourself to do it in 30 minutes. In my training courses, when I talk about productivity, I always say, "Act like you have less time." It works. You can do in 4 hours what you're doing in 8 hours, I guarantee it!

Adults tend to convince ourselves they're bad at learning new things. They think their brains are too old to acquire new skills. The problem is not age, but learning methodology. (Mikel, 2017).

There isn't a secret skill or key that will get you to learn faster. It's not about pressing a button. It will all take time. However, with these methods, you can learn whatever you want with ease.

Start With True Meaning

In order to really understand how something works, then you want to figure out what the true meaning, real intention, and actual purpose of an object, exercise, person, and whatnot. Don't get caught up on superficial descriptions and filler information. Really hone in on what you need to understand about the situation as a whole.

We sometimes try to be too logical. You should approach things like a child, though. Don't overthink and just look at the simple meaning behind a circumstance. Let this be your basis for understanding new information.

Always ask yourself, "Why?" Challenge your intellectual abilities. Go deeper and deeper to discover how various meanings connect to the things that you already know. Understand the intention behind something. What is its true purpose? Why are you doing this?

The more aware you are, the easier it is to remember how things work. This is true for an activity that is as small as learning how to play a dice game or even a more serious one such as operating heavy machinery.

Unfortunately, the school system we know, has always limited people's learning. We were taught to look directly at how to memorize information. Think about it, you always studied to get a good grade, not to really understand the topics.

I want to explain myself better by reporting a small extract from my censored university thesis (2010), so that you can better understand this important concept.

«Each individual develops personal capacities to adapt to reality. These tendencies take many forms, which are sometimes characterized by their effectiveness and inefficiency. For example, a student will prepare differently depending on whether the exam is written or oral, with crosses or open questions, with a good or bad teacher. The grade (if high) will express the effectiveness of the course but not its efficiency. Students give up learning really, preferring the fake recognition of a grade that gives them confidence and the presumption of being superior to other students. However, they will have renounced the attempt to learn.

This paradox (students with higher grades are not always the ones who have learned the most) also extends to the world of work. Employers select their human resources from the wrong principle. The attempt to simplify reality leads them to prefer individuals for their grades (effective path) and not for their skills/abilities (efficient path).

As already explained above, the company recognizes the importance of School for its educational value, but the importance of school is not limited only to the formation of the individual, it also has a direct influence on the economic improvement of society where the link between economy - school - work is inseparable, or at least should be.»

Allow yourself to always understand the deeper meaning or greater truth behind a situation. Don't just memorize information. Instead, understand it in its primordial essence.

The smarter you are, the more you realize how much is left to learn. Sometimes we stop teaching ourselves because we think we don't have to learn anymore. We may stop learning new things and discovering new tools because we feel like we don't need to do this anymore. Don't make that mistake. Keep learning. You'll improve your life on every level.

Keep It Small and Simple

When we learn something new, we often want to do it all at once. No matter what you're learning about, though, you should take your time! There's no rush to accomplish it. Even if the test is the next day, it's better to take your time to understand concepts individually than try to study as hard as possible. What will happen if you have five topics to study and only make it through three? It's better to know these three topics in depth than memorize everything else superficially. First of all because this way you will remember the information better and avoid forgetting it the week after. Then, if you understand one topic, it can become easier to understand the rest as well.

If you were to eat a pizza, it'd be a lot less enjoyable to stick the whole slice in your mouth at once than consume it little by little. When you shove the slice in, you get the pizza at once. However, the aftermath isn't going to be as fun! When you eat it slowly, bite by bite, you appreciate the flavors spreading through your mouth. Your body digests the food easier, too, and it's overall a more pleasant experience that you're likely to remember. Learning works the same. You must slowly savor what you are learning by trying to understand the true meaning of things. And you will give your mind time to digest the concepts better.

Often you might give up learning a new activity because it seems too complicated. The secret is to break down what you have to learn into small parts. Don't imagine a very long road to go. But think of a series of small steps.

If you look at the long road, it may seem difficult, and you may be discouraged. Just focus on the next step. After all, someone who wants to move a mountain will do it stone by stone. You won't try to push the entire mountain from one place to the next all at once. Break your problems down into smaller parts and everything will seem easier.

I would like to conclude with two other concepts. Imagine that you are explaining something to a five-year-old child. From there, you can get into deeper truths and greater meaning.

Finally, never be afraid to ask someone for help when you are learning new information. It may make you feel dumb or less intelligent than others if you have to ask for help. However, truly wise individual in this situation will understand that it's okay to do that. You can visualize a heavy log in the middle of the street that needs to be moved. Is the strong person someone who tries desperately to lift in on their own, unable to even make it budge with their own strength? Or will the smart individual get help from others and guide them in a way that everyone can move the log together with ease?

Unconscious Competence

While understanding things deeply is important, you also need to practice so that you can remember them better.

There are 4 levels of learning. The first level is that of unconscious incompetence. That is, you don't know something exists so you're completely incompetent. The second level is conscious incompetence. You know that thing, but you're incompetent. After the first phase of study and practice, you will arrive at the third level, that of conscious competence. You're starting to get competent. Think of the first times you rode a bike or your first days you drove a car. You paid attention to every single movement you made. You needed your conscious mind to do those things.

But then with constant repetition over time you reach the last level, the level of unconscious competence. This is the level where you can do things automatically, without thinking, this is where everything comes to you spontaneously and naturally. This is the stage where you can achieve mastery. Become a master!

6. Tips for Memory Efficiency

It can be easy to feel as though the brain that we currently have is the one that we'll carry with us forever. This is so far from the truth! Thinking a certain way now doesn't mean that you have to think that way all your life. Just look at how different your mentality is at present from when you were a child!

There will always be parts of yourself that will always be unique. We go through experiences that no one else will ever understand, even if it's a similar situation. This is what we will carry with us and be specific to who we are. Your intelligence can always grow.

Your brain is a tool that you can easily learn to master. You just have to be willing to put the work in!

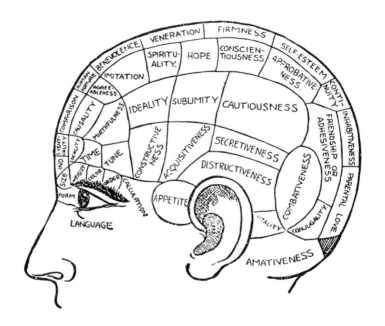

You can create mind palaces. This is a visual way for you to store information. You can create rooms filled with valuable information that you take in. Then, when you need it most, you'll be able to access it easily by traveling through the palace.

To remember little things, some people feel the urge to write on themselves. You may have hands covered in little notes from ink pens or sharpies to help you remember. You shouldn't do this. I want to suggest a better alternative. Let's say you have to remember to mail a letter. Turn your dining room chair backwards. Then, later in the day, you'll see that chair and think, "Why is it like that?" Then, you'll instantly remember that it is a way to remind you to mail the letter.

Make sure you focus on one thing at a time. It can be easy to get sidetracked and lose concentration on the task at hand. Do your best to eliminate distractions, prepare your work environment so that no one can disturb you. Don't move on to the next task until you've finished the first one.

Ensure that you are trying to figure things out before you go asking for help elsewhere. It can be easy to just turn to a friend and ask if they've seen your wallet before looking for it yourself, but always take the hard way and give yourself a mental challenge.

Furthermore, try to use a map before you use a GPS. Look up where you're going beforehand. Print a map out if you want as well so that you can consider getting there without using the GPS. You'll always have your phone as a backup, so you may try challenging yourself. It's also a great exercise to develop a sense of direction. Sometimes it can happen to have downtime. Always have a book to read or one of the games that I have recommended in this book handy. Never waste your time.

Sleep at the Right Time

Sleep is essential not only for your overall health but for your mental well-being as well. This is the time that your brain will be resting, so you must ensure that you are giving your mind this full period of sleep.

A regular cycle is usually good because it means that you will get in balance with your circadian rhythm. Try to go to bed and wake up around the same time every day. Our bodies are on stricter cycles than we may realize, so help them out by having a healthy cycle of sleep.

Your body doesn't always know the difference between a minute or 10; that's why it doesn't have to be something that you stress or panic over. Even if you aim to go to bed between 10 pm to 11 pm every night and wake up between 6 am and 7 am every day, that's okay! The more specific the better, but we can't always live our lives by the last two digits on a clock.

Ensure that you are shutting off electronics long before you plan on falling asleep in addition to this. If you love your brain, don't leave your phone on and charging in the same room where you sleep. Keep it off when you sleep, you'll get a more restorative sleep. And don't make the excuse that you have to leave it on for the alarm clock. Buy one! When you sleep, your cell phone must stay off and in another room. If you can't do it, you have an addiction that you have to treat.

In addition to stress, the excessive use of electronic devices also has a very important impact on brain health.

Try to perform activities during the day to rebalance your cognitive functions, give your brain moments of tranquility and harmony. Like reading, drawing, meditating, having interesting conversations and walking in nature.

Getting exercise during the day can help you sleep better as well. Physical activity improves the quality of sleep. Do something every day to help release physical tension to let your mind relax. Whether it's simply stretching, doing light yoga, or dancing for thirty minutes, this can all help actually relax your body so you can get a deeper sleep.

Too much sleep can actually be bad for you as well. Frequent naps can feel good, but it can leave you groggy and brain-fogged. A nap once a day is fine, but resist the urge to do more than that.

As you are sleeping, it's beneficial to try to keep track of your dreams. This can help you unlock things you didn't know about yourself. Some people will say that they don't dream, but this isn't true. They just don't remember their dreams. The more aware you are of your dream, though, the more you can make it understandable.

Keeping a dream journal increases your creativity. Many scientists and inventors have had brilliant intuitions from their dreams. It is also a great training for your memory as well as being a window into your subconscious.

When you wake up, jot down what just happened. Even if it's a foggy memory, the most important events will stick out to you, and you can remember more about it later.

Write down keywords. Use dream dictionaries and other discussions about dreams to see if there is a deeper meaning behind what you have experienced while sleeping.

The more aware you are of both your conscious and unconscious minds, the easier it will be to take in new information and process it correctly through your memory.

These dreams can also help you to learn more about yourself. Analyze your dreams. This alone makes you analytically and spiritually connected to yourself.

Mindfulness

Mindfulness is a way to keep ourselves connected within this specific moment. It helps us bring attention to the present moment. Often, we can get lost in a fantasy of what may happen in the future. We can get stuck in the past, full of regrets. Mindfulness helps you become aware of this moment and start to see it more clearly. You can remove yourself from the stresses over the past and future so that you can enjoy the present as much as possible.

Living the present means being closer to ourselves. And not abandoning ourselves. It helps us to understand ourselves better. This meditative state is the attainment of self-awareness, of the reality that surrounds us and of the present moment in a non-judgmental way.

You will start to pick up more details. You will realize the actual situation you are in instead of the idea of what you think is going on. In addition to feeling a general sense of physical and mental well-being. Meditation is often associated with mindfulness. After all, they help you understand how to stay within this moment better. For these activities, I'm going to teach you how to easily implement mindfulness into your daily life.

Remember, however, that mindfulness is something you can do anywhere at any time. The more frequently you do it, the easier it will be to stay connected to the present. At first, it may feel weird, but you will eventually be able to stay stuck in the moment, not stressed over the things that you can't control.

Do it when you are feeling anxious. When you find yourself distracted at a party because you're feeling insecure, or you feel like you're about to have a panic attack at work, be mindful. Do one of these exercises.

Practice mindfulness even when you are having a great time. While having fun with your friends, laughing and enjoying yourself, take a second to be mindful and think about how great this experience is. Don't just wait for moments of nervousness before you do that. Practicing it in moments of happiness means really putting into practice the teachings of Horace, who transmitted to us one of the most beautiful values of life: the Carpe Diem.

Soak up everything from each experience, including the bad ones. The more things you take in, the easier it will be to remember all the information that have came along with it. You never know what you may discover when you start paying attention to your current situation.

Pick a Color

For this first mindfulness activity, all that you will have to do is pick a color, texture, shape, or some other physically identifying feature. As an example, let's choose a color.

Start out with green. Pick out everything that's green around you, even if it only has a tinge of it. Make a mental note of it in your head. Perhaps it's a coffee cup sitting on the counter, a keychain on the table, a candle that's half burnt, a plant with wilted leaves, a painting on the wall, or an entire couch. Whatever these items are, choose them because of their color.

That is all you have to do to really stay mindful and connected to what's going on at present. You suddenly become aware of your surroundings and distract yourself from the more anxious thoughts that may have been holding you back.

Work your way through the rest of the colors. Take yourself down the rainbow and repeat it until you are no longer anxious. Once you've done that, choose a texture and pick everything that's wooden.

This will all be enough to distract you from whatever thoughts you're having and keep you in the moment.

This way, you can soak up as much from this situation as possible.

Five Senses

In this case, you are going to focus on tapping into your five senses. We've already discussed how doing so can be helpful in keeping you cognitively stimulated. You will work through your five senses to come to a conclusion about your surroundings. The general rule is to identify anything that can be labeled using one of your senses.

Pick out five things that you can see right in front of you. Say them out loud. If you're not alone, just state them in your head. Maybe it's a TV, a couch, a bed, a chair, and a poster.

Choose four things that you can hear. Perhaps there's a dog barking, a baby crying, a dryer running, or someone's foot tapping. Even if it's not present, what is an object that makes a lot of noise? Maybe there's a guitar in the corner, too.

What are three things that you can touch? You don't have to get up and touch them. Just think about how you can do that and what they may feel like. E.g., a soft carpet, a cat, a knife, or a plant. What two things can you smell? Again, even if you can't smell them right now, such as an unlit candle, identify the objects that you can smell if you want to.

What one thing can you taste? Maybe there's a basket of nuts across the room, a glass of water, or an herb garden.

Just start with the basics and stay logical. However, don't be afraid to pick out things that you can't necessarily taste or smell. Imagine what these smells and flavors may be! This just helps to keep you distracted from anything else that you're thinking about.

Let your ideas get weird as well. You can't eat a couch, but you can certainly taste it if you want. Experiment with these methods of mindfulness and find ways to incorporate more than one of them in your life when you need a distraction from your thoughts.

Body Laser

For this technique, you have to sit or stand up straight. Whether you're sitting down or standing up, just keep your posture as perpendicular to the ground as possible.

Imagine what a laser would have to travel through as it went from the top of your head to the bottom of your toes. Picture it going through your head. It rolls over your eyes, nose, mouth, and chin.

Watch as the laser moves down to your shoulders. It passes over your chest, stomach, and hips. Then, it finishes off through your legs and down to your feet.

When you are feeling stressed, let it pass through the rest of your body. You can visualize the laser to help it travel through your body and stay connected to yourself more than any anxious or stressful thoughts that you're having.

You can also flex these parts of your body and release them in order to keep yourself physically mindful. You may start with your shoulders, stomach, and arms and then move down to your legs and feet. You can flex them for around three seconds at a time and then release. It is something that you can do wherever you are to stay focused on your body.

Reflection Over Anxious Rumination

Stress has physical side effects that can alter your thinking pattern. It can even shape your brain in a different way if you aren't careful about how you manage it.

Rumination is a persistent and depressive form of thinking, a cognitive process characterized by a repetitive style of thought that focuses on negative thoughts and feelings and their negative consequences.

It occurs when you are pondering over every last detail. Maybe you're thinking about a party or hanging onto the smallest embarrassing things that you have said that others do not even remember themselves. Well, don't agonize over what has happened. Keep an objective perspective about the things in your life. Be realistic with your reflection and remember that most people are more judgmental about themselves and their own actions than of what you have said or done. Keep it in mind because if you ruminate too much and stress about the minor details, it can affect how you remember things.

Don't say anything to yourself that you won't say to a

friend. Be kind and remember that the worst thing you've ever done isn't all that bad in the eyes of someone else.

Being negative on yourself isn't the same thing as doing a positive reflection. Whenever you have a negative thought, challenge it with a positive one. If you find that you are reflecting and ruminating too much, then that is the perfect time to pick up some brain games.

When you don't know what to do and are feeling incredibly anxious, envision the advice that you would give to a friend who is in the same situation. Practice self-love and focus on the reality so that you can recall the truth more than the negative aspects.

Memory Minimalism

Minimalism started as an art form in the 1960s. Ever since, minimalism has become a lifestyle. It's often associated with throwing away all your stuff and living with hardly anything. However, it doesn't have to be the case now. It's simply about removing the things you don't need, as well as the ones that don't make you happy.

Cutting down the things you have in your home may help you keep a clear head. If you have a lot of items scattered around the house that don't interest you or serve little purpose, for instance, they can be distracting for you.

When you leave half-finished projects all around the house, it's the same thing as having thoughts left unattended, as well. Even though you may not be thinking about the half-painted desk in the corner, your brain can still visually see it, and it is still using some space to process that information. Let your mind be free and don't keep it cluttered with things that distract you.

When it comes to keeping memories around, make sure that they are what you want anyway. For example, it may be useful to leave thoughts that remind you to achieve your goals. Think of a sheet of paper attached to your bedroom door that you can read when you wake up.

Instead of having a ton of boxes filled with memories, find ways to incorporate them around your house. Hang pictures rather than keep boxes that are filled with them.

Take pictures of objects instead of just keeping them. Having a journal with 100 pictures is a lot less space-consuming than having ten boxes filled with 100 items.

Talking to Intelligent People

We have an intellectual meter that we need to reach. It's important, therefore, to discuss intelligent topics with intelligent people. It's nice to have a bunch of friends whom you can agree with, but you should also look for ways to have friendly debates.

If you don't have people to talk to in real life, the online community is a great way to express yourself.

Just because your friends aren't all scholars doesn't mean that they aren't intelligent enough to have meaningful conversations. Switch the subject matter and what you choose to talk about. Don't gossip about people. Instead, discuss ideas!

Always ask other questions, too. It can be easy to talk about ourselves because that's all that we know. However, be inquisitive and discover the opinions of others. You can learn a lot about yourself by learning about other people.

Being intelligent also means exposing yourself to as much new information as possible. Never turn down an opportunity to learn something fresh.

Game Theory

You're almost done reading this book and I want you to think about game theory, now. This scientific discipline studies the behaviour and decisions of rational subjects in a context of strategic interdependence. This interdependence is the situation in which one individual's choices also influence the choices and situation of other individuals.

Game theory has several implications, one of which is to interpret reality. It helps us understand the logical reasonings that start to develop in our social dynamics. Game theory can also explain how one person may react in a situation and predict what you should do next. Think of a game of chess. You don't just figure out what your next move should be. Instead, you come up with multiple solutions based on what the other person may do as well.

When you understand game theory, you can become more analytical in real life. Always ask yourself why the people around you do what they do and what greater truths it may help you discover.

Conclusion

In order to implement your memory building strategies, make sure that you are actively keeping up with your brain energy and always looking for new ways to grow your mental abilities. Check out the other books in this series for optimal brain strength. The first book is *Photographic Memory*, and the topics include memory techniques and mnemonic strategies. The third book is *Memory Improvement*, and the topics are improving brain health habits to enhance memory, remembering more, and forgetting less.

A big reason why we tend to lose so much information is because we're doing the same thing day after day. Going forward, it is important for your overall health to always choose new ways to try out what you already know.

Your brain is the most important thing you have! Your heart might stop working, but you would still have the potential for a heart transplant. We have yet to determine how to do a full brain transplant. This organ is precious and specific to you. If you don't have good mental well-being, then it can be hard to have improve every other aspect of your life.

Don't be afraid to learn new things! Switch up your life and try activities that scare you. Embrace challenge because it will help you to grow! We only have one life, and we should be doing our best to remember as much as we can to be able to navigate through them. Every boat is safer in the port, but that is not what it was built for.

UPGRADE YOUR MIND -> zelonimagelli.com

UPGRADE YOUR BUSINESS -> zeloni.eu

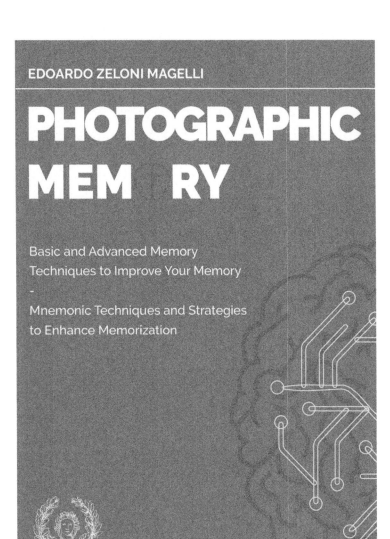

EDOARDO ZELONI MAGELLI

PHOTOGRAPHIC
MEM RY

Basic and Advanced Memory
Techniques to Improve Your Memory
-
Mnemonic Techniques and Strategies
to Enhance Memorization

EDOARDO
ZELONI MAGELLI

EDOARDO ZELONI MAGELLI

MEM●RY IMPROVEMENT

The Memory Book to Improve and Increase
Your Brain Power

-

Brain Food and Brain Health Habits to Enhance
Your Memory, Remember More and Forget Less

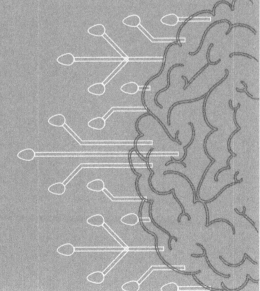

EDOARDO
ZELONI MAGELLI

Bibliographical References

Cherry, K. (2019). *A Simple DIY Short-Term Memory Experiment.* Retrieved from https://www.verywellmind.com/a-short-term-memory-experiment-2795664

Mikel, B. (2017). *Scientists Find an Undeniably Effective Technique for Mastering New Skills.* Retrieved from https://www.inc.com/betsy-mikel/use-this-technique-to-master-a-hard-to-learn-skill-at-any-age.html

Mosconi, L. (2018). *Nutrire il cervello. Tutti gli alimenti che ti rendono più intelligente.*

The Cleveland Clinic. (2017). *Cooking for Cognition: Making a Meal Is Good for Your Brain.* Retrieved from https://healthybrains.org/cooking-cognition-making-meal-good-brain/

Venuti Angelo, Marianetti Massimo, Pinna Silvia (2018). *Allena il tuo cervello. Esercizi, attività e curiosità per tenere in forma la tua mente.*

Wimber, M et al. (2015). Retrieval induces adaptive forgetting of competing memories via cortical pattern suppression. *Nature Neuroscience.*

Zeloni Magelli E. (2010). *La Teoria della Realtà.*

Printed in Great Britain
by Amazon

72463374R00108